CLEAN DISHES CLEAR PROFITS

How to maximise profit through your commercial dishwashing systems

RICHARD HOSE

Foreword by Gary MacLean
MasterChef: The Professionals Winner 2016

D1522243

RETHINK PRESS

First published in Great Britain in 2020
by Rethink Press (www.rethinkpress.com)

Contents

Foreword

Washing dishes! Who cares? Richard Hose cares. Richard not only understands the machines from the ground up, he understands the importance of getting the whole dishwashing system correct the first time. This book is a delightful, informative, and sometimes funny look at the art of warewashing.

In my career I have opened over eighty restaurants, bars and hotels, designing kitchens along the way. As a chef I am happy to say I share Richard's love of a wonderfully designed dishwash area.

My love for such a set up was not instantaneous but forced upon me through many years of working with inadequate dishwash systems. The dishwash area is always a huge pinch point in any kitchen, and I have spent many hours over a sink helping the team to wash dishes because the dishwasher has broken down (again). In my early years I became very good at botching a dishwasher repair, from blocking missing jets with carefully carved cork and butchers string, to hunting B&Q for washers and screws for wash arms. I have seen first-hand how disastrous it can be when you neglect the humble dishwash area. You could say I learned the hard way.

I have found that the function of the washing of dishes tends to be the last thing people think about when designing kitchens. I think it should be the first thing that is on the page when making such an investment in a new food business.

Making best use of space and thinking about every aspect of the operation can pay dividends, touching on things like the quality of the job your machine actually performs, purchasing the correct machine in the first place, looking at staff retention and providing a safe and comfortable workplace for them. Good design and correct purchasing can save not only pounds but a lot of heartache and late nights.

Richard has an encyclopaedic knowledge on all things warewashing. I am sure if you are in the food business you will find this an enjoyable read and an invaluable guide.

Enjoy.

Gary Maclean
Scotland's National Chef, *MasterChef:*
The Professionals **Winner 2016**

Introduction

Clean plates, shiny cutlery and sparkling glasses are your restaurant's calling cards. They are on the front line with your customers and showcase your quality food and drinks. The reputation of your restaurant can hinge on how your customer perceives these. Is it really worth leaving their cleanliness to chance?

Every day, restaurant owners and ambitious chefs face enormous competition when trying to make their restaurant brand stand out from the crowd. A huge amount of effort is involved in setting up and establishing your restaurant as the place where everyone should eat and socialise, and bad reviews can make things very difficult.

Every restaurateur wants to succeed. They want their business to fulfil their dreams and be the success that they dream of. But how does your establishment become just that, and blow the competition out of the water?

The reputation of your restaurant plays a massive part in your success, and I believe that there are a few unsung heroes hiding in the back of your kitchen and behind your bar that are key to that success. Your commercial dishwashing systems and processes deserve a lot more praise than they ever get.

Dirty cutlery, or lipstick on a glass, create an instant negative perception in your customer's mind. When lipstick is found lingering in places where it shouldn't be, it usually results in bags being packed and someone leaving. These could be your clientele if you're not paying enough attention to the cleanliness of your wares.

Between the work that the dishwasher does back of house and your glasswasher at front of house, these humble workhorses play a direct role in helping you to gain new customers and retain your existing regulars. Your dishwashing systems should not be an afterthought or merely adequate.

In *Clean Dishes, Clear Profits* I help you navigate these systems and show you how they can work for your business rather than against it. When wash systems are designed with thought, and your machines treated with care, these powerful allies will reward you time and time again.

How it began

You could ask who cares about commercial dishwashers and glasswashers. Well, I do. I cannot walk into a restaurant, bar/pub/club, café, or any other hospitality-type venue and not try to find out what kind of dishwasher or glasswasher they have and strike up a conversation about it.

It is an obsession that I have that I must share with the people I'm with. I can bore them almost to death with it, so it may be that my compulsion is more life-threatening for those unfortunate few who decide to accompany me on a night out! Luckily for them, I'm married with children, so these night outs are getting further and further apart! My poor, long-suffering wife however, continues to endure with an amused smile.

My earliest introduction to the function and power of commercial ware washing systems and machinery was when I was a student working part-time for a large hospitality subcontractor. It was in Scotland's home of rugby, Murrayfield in Edinburgh.

One of my first jobs was working in a wash area that complimented the corporate suits that acted as hospitality for thousands of delegates during match days.

I was a kitchen porter (KP) and whenever there was a home game, we would be responsible for the quick turnaround of hundreds of clean dishes between courses. The results on the rugby field, however, were not always as good as the results we produced in those wash areas, which circumnavigated the stadium and helped create an unforgettable experience for the lucky delegates.

It was a baptism of fire which has stayed with me ever since. I've never feared a hard shift and although it was difficult work, it was rewarding. There was a correct way to achieve success, and to maximise our time and carry it out efficiently, but there were also plenty of wrong ways. Over time, and with experience and guidance, we got better at refining the system to get the clean crockery back into the kitchen for re-plating. It certainly held me in good stead for a career in later life that has now become my passion.

Later, when I started working in our industry full time, this invaluable experience would be called upon to help other venues to tweak and improve their dishwashing and glasswashing systems.

Back in the early 2000s, I was fortunate enough to visit family in South Africa on an amazing three-week-long holiday. The trip was incredible. We were able to take in a safari adventure, sail in a boat alongside a family of southern right whales, and cage dive with great white sharks, among the many highlights.

In Cape Town, at the top of their world-famous Table Mountain, there is a café that provides refreshments for the tourists that visit. After we abseiled off the side of the mountain, we ate in the café and talked about our day. I don't know what model they have now, but back then they had a top-of-the-range commercial passthrough dishwasher by a well-known manufacturer. It was in their back kitchen but was visible from the counter area where you ordered and collected your food. I had a chuckle to myself that I was now starting to seek out the models that different establishments had, and this has never left me. I know, it takes all kinds...

I came back into the hospitality industry as a salesman of commercial dishwashers and glasswashers. As part of my training, I worked for six months with the dishwasher engineer so that I intimately understood the internal workings of the machines that I would be selling.

After two years the engineer left the company and I fell into the role of sales and service engineer. I remained in this role until 2010, when I set up my own business. Since then, my team and I have made it our mission to 'make life easier' for the staff in professional kitchens, by transforming underperforming wash areas into sleek 'battle stations' that realise profit for the chef and restaurant owner.

The good news for you is that this obsession translates quite easily into a useful step-by-step system, with great hints and tips, that will transform an underperforming dishwash system into a better performing, slicker operation.

My years of experience in this field will help you to overcome most barriers and problems that come with running a busy kitchen when the dishwasher is underperforming.

Every kitchen that prepares and serves food from non-domestic premises should be using a commercial dishwasher to clean and sanitise their dishes. Every place that serves drinks in a non-domestic environment should have a commercial glasswasher to clean and rinse their glassware.

The range of establishments that the previous statement covers is vast. You could run a pub or restaurant, a grand hotel, a children's nursery, a school, or a church hall. Regardless of what your place is, or how it is categorised, you will find this book useful. To keep things simple, I will narrow this down and refer to it as a restaurant environment. The principles and steps involved will be relevant to any commercial kitchen.

Where glasswashers are concerned, I will go into more detail about the specifics of these too. Again, the principles will be similar, but there are a few points which differ and need clarification.

For readers that are starting a restaurant project from scratch, you will find this easy-to-follow methodology helps immeasurably when planning your new business. This book contains information to help you plan and execute a great bar and kitchen wash-up area.

When this is done correctly, it will have a positive impact on your restaurant's profit margin. This book will give you the strategies, insights, and tools you need to achieve this. It may seem like a bold assertion but read on and you will see why I'm making such a claim.

You want to make your restaurant unique and stand out from the crowd. It may be that the food you offer is different; it may be that the layout and décor is quirky and eye-catching. It may be that you have a similar offering to that of your competition but your method of delivery and the staff you have employed make it the place that customers want to eat in.

Along with great staff that you have carefully hired, you have a wonderful kitchen and bar setup that beautifully brings it all together and keeps your customers raving and coming back for more.

You are fully booked, your diary has a waiting list, and Google and TripAdvisor are brimming with 5-star reviews. This is the dream. How close are you to this dream? There already? Almost there? Or is it still a far-off fantasy?

There are restaurants and chefs that are achieving this dream daily, but how do they do it? There is not one correct answer to this question. There are various factors that must be right in order to achieve this.

One of these factors is their bar and kitchen dishwashing system. I strongly believe that these systems are crucial in the success of any great restaurant, and that if they have been planned, properly thought out, and are well looked after, they will reward the restaurateur many times over.

This may seem boring and a far cry from what any Michelin-starred restaurant would want to concentrate their energy on but I promise you that giving this area the correct amount of attention will have a positive impact on your bottom line.

I aim to educate and inspire you to view these systems as the vital assets that they are. If you implement even some of the information in this book, then there is a high chance that you will no longer be faced with avoidable expensive engineer repair calls. That alone will make it worthwhile, and ultimately, it will make life easier for you and will take you closer to achieving your dream.

The fact that you are reading this book shows that you care or are at least intrigued about how important dishwashing systems are to a hospitality establishment. The book is not aimed at kitchens that are satisfied with meeting the bare minimum in standards. This is not to criticise establishments where budget is tight or new starts that must account for every penny spent. Rather, it reflects that I have always tried to get a dishwasher working beyond environmental health standards, and have the machine performing at its best.

In my experience, there are only a handful of unscrupulous business owners that are unwilling to spend money to have their machines repaired properly, and they always buy the cheapest ware washer they can get. Simply put, you get what you pay for. This covers both sales and service and sooner rather than later it unravels to reveal a waste of money and the old adage 'if you buy cheap you buy twice' comes true.

Thankfully, most restaurant owners see the value in good service and products and how it enhances their business. If this sounds more like the way you operate, then read on and enjoy.

You will benefit from reading this book cover to cover. However, when used as a reference book and guide it will still provide you with relevant information as you dip in and out of it over time. It is not meant to be exhaustive in its description of various components, machines, and parts; it is written as a practical and helpful guide.

The five-step methodology is the main part of this book, and this is where the real magic happens. I delve into geek mode in certain sections about how critical a piece of information is and should you decide to read through (and you are strongly advised to do so) then you will be rewarded with a great bit of info that will open your eyes and change the way you perceive your machine.

Some of the 'mistakes your staff are making' may seem like common sense to you or me, but trust me, you will be surprised at what some staff can get up to when you are not around. And you never know, my obsession might be contagious. I may one day find myself inundated with pictures and information about where you've spotted machines in far-flung places on your travels.

So, congratulations for picking up this book. You are one step closer to gaining more profit in your restaurant. Read on and enjoy!

PART ONE

WHY YOU NEED A DISHWASH SYSTEM

1
What Are Ware Washers?

Restaurants have a high throughput of dirty plates, crockery, cutlery, cups, saucers, glasses, and prep equipment coming in and out of their kitchen during service. Commercial dishwashers and glasswashers are needed to sanitise and kill germs and bacteria. These machines perform a high temperature wash and a sanitising rinse which prevents cross-contamination and leaves the plates, cups, and cutlery ready to be used again. This is the basic but vital purpose that they serve.

However, commercial dishwashers are more than just this function. Over the decades since their inception, they have evolved to meet the needs of a busy kitchen and bar and the right equipment in the right place can transform how a bar and restaurant operates.

The first dishwashers

The idea of the dishwasher is not new. In fact, it was over a century and a half ago that the first dishwasher was invented and received its first patent. This was as far back as 1850 when Joel Houghton created his version of one.[1] His manual machine consisted of a hand-turned wheel that splashed water onto dishes although unfortunately, it wasn't effective at cleaning them.

Credit for inventing the first working automatic dishwasher goes to Mrs Josephine Cochrane (1839–1913), of Shelbyville, Illinois.[2] She was frustrated by her staff constantly chipping and breaking her fine china, so she took matters into her own hands. Josephine worked at various designs and finally got help with the construction of a dishwasher from mechanic George Butters and received her first patent on the Garis-Cochrane Dish-Washing Machine on December 28, 1886.

Her dishwasher was a wooden tub with a wire basket in it – the dishes went in the basket, and rollers rotated the dishes. As a handle on the tub was turned, hot, soapy water was sprayed into the tub, cleaning the dishes. Cochrane's machine was first shown at the 1893 World's Fair in Chicago, Illinois. Initially, her

---

1   Kate Hilpern (2010) 'The Secret History of the Dishwasher', www.independent.co.uk/life-style/gadgets-and-tech/features/the-secret-history-of-the-dishwasher-2119320.html
2   Debbie Foulkes (2010) 'Josephine Cochrane (1839–1913) Invented the Dishwasher', forgottennewsmakers.com/2010/04/20/josephine-cochrane-1839-1913-invented-the-dishwasher

machine was only bought by some restaurants and hotels, and so the commercial dishwasher was officially born.

In 1912, at 73 years old, Cochrane was still personally selling her machines. She died in 1913 and her legacy has lived on ever since though the dishwasher didn't become widespread as a labour-saving machine in households until the 1960s.

In the guise of a stainless-steel box, the humble dishwasher takes on many forms. The collective name for this type of machine is a ware washer. This covers both glasswashers and dishwashers of varying shapes and sizes. Put simply, it is a machine that washes the wares in your establishment.

There are countless makes and models out in the marketplace which all stake their own claim at being the best, most affordable, most efficient, most sustainable, etc – but more on this later. At their core, the primary function is to clean and sanitise dishes, cutlery, cups, glasses (the wares) so that they can be reused throughout your restaurant's service and minimise the breakages that come with hand washing.

The term 'ware washing equipment' covers quite a large amount of commercial cleaning equipment. This machinery includes glasswashers; frontloading or undercounter dishwashers; passthrough dishwashers; rack conveyor dishwashers; flight dishwashers; and pot, pan, and utensil washers. There are variations on some of these machines, as well as tray washers and crate washers for specialist areas in certain industries.

In a restaurant, the ware washing machine setup usually consists of glasswashing and dishwashing. In larger setups there will be a pot wash area and occasionally a pot wash machine. Let's have a look at the variations of these machines, their general components, and what function these play within the ware washer.

Glasswashers

Glasswashers are typically behind or off to the side of the bar and are normally frontloading machines. The door opens at the front, the glass basket is loaded, and the door is closed for the cycle to be activated (button control start). Frontloading machines are also known as under counter models, for the obvious reason that they are sited under the countertop of a bar.

Glasswashers come in various sizes. For ease of identification, these are referred to by the size of the square basket/rack that fits into the machine:

- Small – 350mm² basket. Accommodates nine to twelve pint glasses.

- Medium – 400mm² basket (and sometimes 450mm² basket). Accommodates twelve to sixteen pint glasses.

- Large – 500mm² basket. Accommodates sixteen to twenty-five pint glasses.

This is a rough rule of thumb and, of course, depends on what type of glasses you are using. If you have a tie-in with a brewery, then this might not be your decision. They may dictate to you what glasses you should be using to serve their drinks.

There are still open glasswashers on the market that are sometimes referred to as the hedgehog-style glasswashers. The brushes on these machines spin mechanically in a solution of lukewarm water and detergent and glasses are manually dipped in and out of the liquid and brushes then set aside to dry. These machines are in decline as they are quite labour intensive and they don't wash and rinse in high temperatures. However, they have been useful in the past where space is an issue in a small bar because they could sit discreetly in a corner.

Now and again I have been asked to supply a slim-line commercial dishwasher. These do not exist in the commercial space. Someone will have done an internet search and seen a smaller 400mm² basket-sized glasswasher, and may have read the word 'dishwasher'. This term was put in to help with internet search engine rankings but should not be there. It is the same when they are referred to as 'bar dishwashers'.

You will struggle to get any 400mm² baskets with pegs to hold dinner plates. They tend to come with a supply of flat baskets for glasses with a small insert to handle small saucers. The industry standard for a commercial dishwasher basket size is a 500 × 500mm² basket.

I have customers ask us to come look at their dishwasher and when the engineer turns up on-site, it is often their glasswasher that they are referring to. We try and build this into our questioning so that we are better prepared for the site repairs, and ask: 'Do you mean the dishwasher in the kitchen or the glasswasher behind the bar?' It helps us to clarify what we're going to help with.

Glasswashers can't be used as dishwashers and vice versa unless the working temperatures are modified by an engineer. Glasswasher temperatures are not high enough for dishes and dishwasher temperatures are too high for glasses.

Glasswasher temperatures are factory set to wash at 55°C and rinse at 70°C. This side of the industry is not as strict with temperatures because there is no food involved and a low chance of E. coli being present.

If glasses are washed at too high a temperature over long periods of time it will weaken the glass and lead to breakages, both inside and outside the machine. This is prevalent when there is a shortage of glasses during a busy period and they are taken straight from the machine and filled with ice or a cold drink. The immediate extreme changes in temperature can shatter the glass. This is a hazard for bar staff and is something to watch out for. Industrial glasswashers are extremely important in a bar, club, or restaurant, and savvy staff will recognise and appreciate the job that they do to help them during and after a busy service.

2
Dishwashers

Commercial dishwashers must clean and sanitise dirty plates, which have the remains of food particles on them. In the UK these machines are built to a certain standard to deal with the remains of food particles. They must stop bacterial cultures from growing and minimise any risk to public health, and as such, there are certain features and functions that each manufacturer includes.

Dishwashers are set to wash the dishes between 55–65°C and then rinse them at least at 82°C. This high rinse temperature is for environmental health purposes and it is higher than the danger zone within which bacteria grows.

Surprisingly, there is no specific food safety legislation that states that you need to have a commercial dishwasher in your premises. The government has produced guides to prevent cross-contamination within section 3 of the current E.coli 0157 guidance documents.[3] Realistically, you need a commercial dishwasher to achieve these temperatures and serve more than a few customers.

Each machine must be fitted with a Water Regulations Advisory Scheme (WRAS) approved air gap.[4] This is a physical gap which exists between the fresh water supply feeding into the dishwasher from your mains water. Its purpose is to avoid the backflow of dirty, contaminated dish water into the public water mains system.

If your dishwasher does not have a WRAS approved air gap, then you are putting yourself and others at risk by operating such a machine. If something goes wrong and your machine contaminates the drinking water of your town, it will be highly unlikely that your insurance would cover such an outcome if this basic dishwasher part was not fitted as standard. Heed this

---

3   E.coli guidance for Scotland: www.foodstandards.gov.scot/
     publications-and-research/publications/ecoli-o157-control-of-cross-
     contamination; E.coli guidance for the UK: www.food.gov.uk/
     business-guidance/e-coli-cross-contamination-guidance; Cooksafe
     manual: www.foodstandards.gov.scot/publications-and-research/
     publications/cleaning-schedule
4   Water Regulations Advisory Scheme: www.wras.co.uk/resources/
     glossary/air_gap

as a warning against cheap imported machines. Carry out your due diligence.

The dishwasher cycle

With frontloading and passthrough dishwashers, there are variations in how a complete cycle is achieved but it is normally as follows:

- Wash

- Drain

- Rinse

Wash

The machine starts the process with a powerful wash cycle. Using the water in the dishwasher wash tank, hot water ranging in temperature from 55–65°C is pumped around the wash system and over the dirty dishes via the wash pump and wash arms. When there is a basket full of plates in the dishwasher, the top wash arm sprays the water down onto the front of the plates (because they sit at a slight angle), and the bottom wash arm sprays the wash water upwards and onto the backs of the plates.

Through the power of the wash pump, the wash water is forced along these arms and through small wash arm jets which then spray the water in an even manner. The wash arms rotate with the power of the wash pump so that there is total coverage of wash water over the dishes throughout the wash cycle.

This agitation is combined with commercial dishwasher detergent which helps loosen the soil and food particles on the wares. The chemical detergent holds the soil in suspension during the wash cycle. The wash cycle will last forty-five seconds to a few minutes. This depends on the model of machine, the programme selected, the power of the wash pump, and whether the machine has a thermostop control on the main circuit board.

Drain

The next stage is for three litres of existing wash water to be drained off. This varies depending on the machine and how much water the wash tank holds. This process of draining down some of the wash tank water removes the dirty water from the tank and creates a lower volume of water in the wash tank, so it does not overflow in the rinse stage.

Rinse

The final rinse is extremely important. This fresh water comes from the boiler of the dishwasher and travels through on a separate system from the wash system. It is heated to at least 82°C, which in the UK means that it is rinsing at environmental health standards in order to kill any bacteria. In some countries, including the US, sanitisation is achieved at lower temperatures and by means of chemical sanitation.

The rinse arms are thinner and are located at the top of the wash tank spraying downwards, and at the bottom of the wash tank spraying upwards. These arms rotate with either the pressure from the incoming fresh water to refill the boiler, or from the pressure of the rinse boost pump where the water pressure is poor or an air gap has been fitted (in the latter case there is no pressure from the mains water inside of the machine). Like the wash arms, the rinse arms have small jets along their length which concentrate the force of the rinse water over the dishes, giving total coverage.

Chemical rinse aid is injected into the boiler and mixes with the final rinse. The rinse aid contains ingredients to sanitise the dishes and disperse the water from the surface of the wares so they dry quicker. Once the full cycle is complete and the dishes are removed, they dry quickly. This drying time varies depending on the suitability of the rinse aid used.

Dishwasher – front loader

Similar in size to the larger glasswashers, front loaders have the same physical footprint as a domestic dishwasher or washing machine. They measure w × d × h = 600 × 600 × 820mm, which is the industry standard.

As the name suggests, they open at the front and the basket loaded with dishes is pushed into the wash chamber. The door is closed and the machine is put through a wash cycle. These machines are also known as under counter dishwashers and are great in smaller kitchens and cafés where space is at a premium and the volume of throughput is not too high. On average they can handle thirty to forty racks per hour.

Sitting under the worktop counter provides the staff with more space to carry out kitchen duties such as prep work. However, when planning an under counter setup, remember to allow workspace for dirty dishes, filling dishwasher baskets, and space for clean dishes to sit and be unloaded.

Dishwasher – passthrough

Also known as a hood type dishwasher, the passthrough dishwashers are more suited to busier sites where a higher throughput is required. They can accommodate sixty to seventy racks per hour. They require more kitchen space than the undercounter model as stainless-steel tabling can be hooked on at either side to run the basket of dishes through from one side to the other.

Passthrough dishwashers are set up as a straight through operation or in the corner. Either way, there will be inlet and outlet tabling at each side of it. These should be consistent with the flow of the kitchen running (dirty to dishwasher to clean) and set up left to right or right to left accordingly.

'Fill and dump' machines

These machines still perform a wash, drain, and rinse cycle, but the way it's carried out is different. These machines fill up the wash tank with hot water from the boiler and wash the dishes in this water while mixing with detergent. The dirty wash water is then dumped down the drain. The machine refills the wash tank from the boiler and brings in rinse aid. This acts as the dishwasher rinse and the cleaning cycle is complete. The next cycle uses this rinse water (mixed with detergent which is automatically pumped in) for the wash and then dumps it out. This process repeats.

This is older technology in the UK as it uses more water per cycle than the newer style of machines. This style of machine is still popular in the US. They use chemical sanitiser to kill the bacteria as the rinse is not usually as hot on this type of dishwasher. However, it is a good method of cleaning the dishes and although the lower operating temperatures can save money on heating, the chemical sanitiser (predominantly chlorine-based) is harmful to aquatic life and our environment.

Dishwasher – conveyor

The conveyor dishwasher is designed for higher-volume premises where a fast throughput of a few thousand dishes per hour is necessary. It is physically larger than a standard passthrough dishwasher and is sometimes referred to as a rack conveyor dishwasher. The smallest is equivalent to two or three 500mm² baskets in length and the largest can fill a room at lengths of 5 or 6 metres.

These machines are specified as either a left to right flow or a right to left flow of operation. It is imperative to know this prior to installation as it cannot be changed to suit. The only other option is to change your whole system to work in reverse. The implications of getting this wrong would be with the tabling and sinks, as they would have to be renewed to suit.

With a frontloading dishwasher and a passthrough dishwasher, there is a door to open or hood to lift to insert the basket into the machine. However, with a conveyor machine there is no door or hood to open or lift. The operator pushes the loaded basket into the opening of the conveyor machine and the basket catches onto metal legs or levers. The basket is pulled through automatically on a mechanised conveyor system. There are plastic curtains at the opening and at the clean side of the machine, which cut down on splashing and help retain the hot temperatures within the machine.

Smaller versions of a conveyor dishwasher consist of a single wash tank and a rinse area. The basket is pulled through the wash area and then into the rinse chamber and out the other end.

On larger machines this is more sophisticated. Large machines are great for an outside catering or events company when hundreds of guests attend and the plates can't be washed on-site at the venue, or even on that same day. The crockery, cutlery, and glasses are packed away and transported back to the caterer's premises to be washed.

When dirty dishes are stacked together and allowed to dry, they become harder to clean, because both the front and the back of each plate is soiled. In these circumstances, the larger conveyor dishwashers come into their own.

The operator loads the plates into a basket, gives them a quick wet with the pre-spray tap and pushes them into the machine. The first stage is a prewash which soaks the plate and loosens the dirt. The next stage is the actual wash where the soil is further loosened, and combined with detergent, high wash temperature, and long wash contact time. Then the wares move into the rinse chamber.

The rinse takes away any remaining soil and detergent and sanitises the plates with a minimum 82°C rinse water temperature. Rinse aid within the rinse water starts to disperse water from the surface of the plates. Finally, the conveyor moves the basket into a drying tunnel which ensures that when the plates exit the machine, they are clean, sanitised, dry and ready to be packed away for the next event.

Because the conveyor mechanism is constantly on when the baskets are inserted into the front end of the machine, when they exit the dishwasher, they are pushed along the exit table until they reach the end of the table. In order to prevent the baskets from being forced out when there is no more room for them, and to avoid the conveyor motor from burning out, a stop end switch is fitted to the end of the exit tabling. When a basket bumps into this switch, it signals to the conveyor system to stop. An operator would then unload the baskets until there is room again for more baskets.

Without one of these machines, you would need multiple staff carrying out various roles and the process would be extremely labour intensive, especially when having to dry everything to be packed away again.

Dishwasher – flight machine

From a layman's perspective, a flight dishwasher is similar in design to a conveyor dishwasher although they can be longer in length. The flight machine is more like an actual, continuous conveyor system that runs from one end of the machine to the other and back to the start. Plates are loaded directly onto rows of hard plastic pegs and are drawn into the machine. If you imagine the way that escalators work, where the stairs continuously move in the same direction on a loop system, then a flight dishwasher operates under the same principle.

A flight dishwasher has all the trappings of a large conveyor and sometimes more – prewash, wash, pre-rinse, rinse, and drier. Some of these machines are massive and are used in large-scale operations such as motorway service station restaurants, airports, prisons, and hospitals. The operator stacks the clean wares straight onto trolleys to be taken away. They do not have the 'inconvenience' of having to first load a basket or empty a basket of clean dishes at the other side.

Pot wash/utensil wash

For washing pots and large kitchen items like gastronorm trays, large double sinks can be used. A dedicated pot wash machine is employed for heavier operations. These have heavy-duty wash pumps and can handle the toughest of cleaning jobs. The pot wash, utensil wash, or pan wash comes as a single or double tank machine.

Some manufacturers developed these to use plastic pellets to do the cleaning. The pumps fire thousands of small plastic pellets at the inside of the trays or pots to be cleaned and this aggressive approach attacks the burned-on dirt and food residue and 'pings' it off.

The job of a commercial dishwasher is simple, but over the years the way that this process is delivered to the restaurant owner has resulted in a sophisticated machine that is sometimes over-engineered. The purpose behind this is to achieve more than just clean dishes and we'll cover this later in our five-step methodology.

3

Understanding
The Machine

Arguably the most complicated piece of machinery in a commercial kitchen, a typical dishwasher can work solidly from 7am in the morning through to midnight, seven days a week, every day of the year. It is imperative that the correct machine is chosen from the outset, otherwise it will provide nothing but headaches throughout its lifetime.

Your ware washer is an integral part of the well-oiled machine that is your restaurant. It is as vital as the oven that cooks the food and the fridges that keep the food cool. If you understand how difficult things can get when this 'cog' in the works is neglected and underappreciated, then you will undoubtedly realise the benefits that a well-run dishwasher system will bring to your business.

In my experience, the dishwasher is only thought about after it breaks down and then it is sorely missed. If you understand the components and how dishwashers are put together, you will realise that they should be looked after.

I often get service calls that go something like this:

'Hi, can you send an engineer out to fix our dishwasher please?'

'What has gone wrong with it?'

'I've had the handyman look at it and he said the pump has gone in it.'

'Did he say which pump has gone?'

'No. He just said that the pump is no longer working and will need replacing.'

This is a common conversation. I explain that we need to inspect the machine before ordering any parts because there are five different pumps inside an average dishwasher and we need to determine which one has become faulty. This information usually takes people by surprise. They fail to realise that the dishwasher is a complex piece of machinery. It's not until it breaks down and chaos ensues that everyone suddenly notices its importance.

Internals and externals

The five pumps that are inside your average machine are the:

- Wash pump

- Rinse boost pump

- Drain pump

- Detergent pump

- Rinse aid pump

Some of the larger machines that were described earlier may have more than one wash pump, rinse boost pump, and drain pump.

Wash pump

The wash pump carries out the wash cycle by circulating the wash water through the wash system, through both top and bottom wash arms, and back into the wash tank. This is repeated many times throughout the wash cycle. Wash pumps are the largest of the pumps and have a powerful motor which forces the water through the system. They work off either a three-phase electrical supply or a single-phase supply, depending on the setup of the dishwasher itself and the site.

There is a filter at the entrance to the wash pump which can be removed for regular cleaning. Its purpose is to stop larger food scraps and debris from entering the face of the wash pump and clogging it up. If this happens and is not addressed, the wash pump motor will be unable to turn and will overheat and cut out. If the wash pump has a thermal cut off to protect the motor, it can handle this a few times. Some motors do not have thermal cut offs and end up burning out. The wash pump is one on the most expensive parts to replace in a commercial dishwasher.

Rinse boost pump

Critical in delivering the final rinse in a dishwasher cycle, the rinse boost pump also fills the wash tank. Once the water in the boiler reaches the required transfer temperature, it needs to be 'boosted' up into the wash tank in order to fill the machine. The rinse boost pump carries out this function. Relying on the water pressure through the fill solenoid is no longer an option as water regulations in the UK dictate that a physical air gap must be present in all industrial dishwashers. This ensures that if the machine develops a fault, then dirty water from the machine cannot backflow and re-enter the freshwater system and contaminate the local supply.

Drain pump

During each cycle, the drain pump is activated either once the wash cycle has completed, or when the rinse cycle is done. Its purpose is to drain off some of the wash water so that when the final rinse is executed, the wash tank water level does not become too high.

At the end of the daily shift or mid-afternoon once the lunch period has subsided, the dishwasher should be put through a drain cycle and emptied down. The machine can then be cleaned and refilled before the next service starts.

Not all dishwashers have a drain pump, and this is when the machine can use gravity to drain away. If the external plumbing (the white waste plumbing pipes behind or to the side of the machine) is lower than the wash tank of the machine, then the dishwasher can be specified without a drain pump.

This means that there is a standpipe (or drain plug) inside the wash tank of the machine and when the water volume becomes higher than this standpipe, the excess water runs away into the waste system and the tank level is maintained. Draining down at the end of the shift means pulling out the standpipe/plug and letting the water drain.

A frontloading dishwasher with a gravity drain setup usually sits on a metal stand. This setup is becoming less common in the industry as manufacturers move towards a one-size-fits-all-location machine where they have a drain pump fitted as standard, and volume of throughput is a more dominant factor.

Make sure that your staff do not remove the drain or wash pump filters until after the machine has been drained down. They can then see if there are any large pieces of food, spoons, juice caps, etc lying in the empty wash tank or filters. This debris can be discarded before the filters are removed for cleaning. This is the number one cause of drain pumps becoming blocked, and is avoidable through better staff training.

Filters

Filters are designed to collect food debris that has not been properly pre-scraped before entering the machine. They protect the wash pump, drain pump, and the wash and drain systems from getting clogged up. Not all filters are fully effective and they improve in more sophisticated machines. Make sure your staff know where the filters should be situated and when and how to remove them for daily cleaning.

Ensure that staff can fit the filters back in place correctly and know which part of the filter is up and which is down. If the filters are put in upside down and the machine kicks into a wash cycle, the wash pump is powerful enough to draw the filter in and this forces the wash pump to labour unnecessarily. This leads to the wash pump burning out.

The filters are not there as a major line of defence against food scraps. Your dishwasher is not a waste disposal system. Soft food particles can be drawn through the filters and through the wash system where they collect in the wash arms and end up blocking the wash jets. This renders the final wash results as unacceptable.

Check these points regularly. I've been to new glass-washers where the manager is convinced their four-week-old machine is ineffective and they regret buying it. They claim that the staff are constantly cleaning it out but to no avail. We get on-site and investigate only to discover that the filter has never once been removed and is covered in four weeks' worth of debris.

The best machines pride themselves in their multi-layer filter systems which are highly effective, maintain hygiene, and are easily accessible for staff. They work great when cleaned regularly and are fitted back in properly. Any broken or damaged filters should be replaced as soon as possible. I've lost count of the number of things that I've pulled out of wash pumps and drain pumps over the years, with the main contender probably being teaspoons.

Again, check regularly that these points are understood by your staff.

Detergent pump

The detergent pump is normally a peristaltic pump which draws chemical liquid detergent from the chemical container through tubing (which may be clear or colour coded) and into the wash tank of the dishwasher. This pump is activated during the initial fill of the machine when the dishwasher is first switched on and then it tops up the detergent level during every cycle. The volume of detergent needed can be calibrated by adjustments made on the pumps or at the dishwasher control panel.

Another method on larger machines is to use a detergent probe that is fitted within the wash tank. This probe measures the conductivity of the wash water and determines if the detergent needs to be topped up in accordance with pre-set parameters on the dosing unit. They work well but need to be cleaned often. Depending on the type of probe and its location, your staff may be able to clean it. Otherwise the dishwasher or chemical engineer can carry out this task.

Rinse aid pump

The rinse aid pump will be a peristaltic pump, a diaphragm pump, or a solenoid pump which injects the rinse aid liquid into the rinse boiler prior to the final rinse at the end of the dishwasher cycle. The quality and concentration of rinse aid varies across our industry and the good ones only require a small amount in each cycle. The volume of rinse aid taken in can be adjusted at the pump level or the machine control panel, depending on the make/model of the dishwasher and pump.

Sometimes the chemical pumps are set up externally to the dishwasher by the chemical supplier. This type of setup is known as an external chemical dosing unit. A few chemical companies fit their own systems, known as solid systems, which are powdered chemicals mixed with water. These are then injected into the machine.

Dishwasher tabling

The tabling for a dishwasher is constructed of stainless steel on the working surfaces with milder steel legs and frame. Austenitic stainless steels are used in commercial kitchens and have 16% to 26% chromium and as much as 35% nickel content. This steel is non-ferrous and not magnetic. The usual thickness is up to 2mm and will be either 304 or 316 AISI grade.

Stainless steel is a great material as it doesn't rust easily, is highly durable, and can withstand abuse in a commercial setting. It is easy to keep clean, hygienic and will last decades. A special way to shine it up (on non-food surfaces) is to spray on WD-40 or baby oil and polish it – it will look like new. It can bring a dull, tired-looking dishwasher back to life.

Inlet tabling

The inlet tabling for a commercial passthrough dishwasher can be positioned at the front or either the left- or right-hand side, dependent on the direction of flow of dirty to clean dishes. The inlet tabling is where the dirty dishes are introduced to the machine. It is ideal if there is a set-down area for dirty dishes at the start of the inlet tabling.

A typical inlet setup has at least one sink and sometimes two, an overhead pre-spray with faucet tap, a boxed edge to accommodate the baskets, and an undershelf. There is usually a high splashback set behind the pre-spray or taps to prevent water running down the wall to the rear.

Outlet tabling

The dishwasher outlet tabling for a passthrough model can sit at the front, left-, or right-hand side of the machine and is positioned at a right angle to the inlet tabling (corner setup) or at a 180° angle to the inlet tabling (straight through setup). Outlet tabling also has a boxed edge to allow the basket to flow out of the machine and consists of a bank of runners for basket storage or an undershelf or both.

There are different designs and variations of dishwasher tabling and as such, it's always a good idea to get new ideas from other restaurants or suppliers or speak to your local stainless steel fabricator. The side nearest the dishwasher in both the inlet and outlet tabling is bent down and 'lips' into the machine to ensure a smooth run for the basket and to prevent water from dripping onto the floor.

Although primarily designed for sites with larger operations, I find that passthrough dishwashers are a welcome addition to church kitchens. The church halls are not too busy in their volume of dishes, but where most of the staff are a bit older in age, they prefer the convenience of sliding the baskets through the dishwasher as opposed to lifting it down from a countertop and into a frontloading dishwasher. When a frontloading dishwasher has completed a cycle and the dishes are clean, the heavy basket must be lifted back out and up onto the countertop again. A passthrough dishwasher is preferred in these establishments.

Rack (basket)

The plastic tray which holds the wares to be washed inside the dishwasher is known as either the dishwasher 'rack' or 'basket'. They mean the exact same thing. The industry standard size for a dishwasher basket is 50 × 50cm or 500mm² (19¾″ × 19¾″). The side height of the baskets is generally around 100mm high.

Peg basket

The peg basket is primarily for plates. They normally consist of rows of plastic peg uprights with nine sections which can accommodate two large dinner plates on each row. This means that eighteen dinner plates can be washed in each basket at the one time. Cups and mugs can fit over and around these pegs. Don't be tempted to place cutlery lying flat in these peg baskets as the cutlery will fall through the spaces on the floor of the basket, and down into the wash tank of the machine. Worse still, the cutlery will become stuck and this will stop the wash and rinse arms from rotating.

Flat basket

The flat baskets are ideal for cups, mugs, and large utensils. They are not suitable for plates as they can't stand up in this type of basket. There are no pegs for the plate to rest against.

Cutlery basket

The cutlery basket comes in two different types – a horizontal stack rack and a vertical stack insert basket. The horizontal stack rack is like the flat basket described above except the base of the basket consists of a tighter criss-cross mesh which stops cutlery from falling through (even teaspoons). These are good when there isn't a great deal of cutlery being washed. If there is a larger volume, the cutlery tends to get thrown in and layered on top of each other and it is difficult for the wash water and rinse water to have a proper effect on all sides of the cutlery.

I recommend using a vertical stack cutlery basket which is half the size of a standard basket. This basket rests inside a flat basket and you can fit two side by side in a standard flat basket. Each has six to eight compartments and the cutlery is stacked vertically in each compartment. It is good practice not to overload each compartment so that the wash and rinse can work well.

I remember trialling a new rinse aid on a conveyor dishwasher in a college. They were a relatively large operation with hundreds of dishes and cutlery hitting the wash area over the lunchtime period. They did not have an automatic drier at the clean end of their rack conveyor and could not afford any time for the clean wares to sit and air dry before going back into service again. It was the first time that I'd seen how effective the correct cutlery basket was combined with the correct rinse aid. When the dishes and cutlery exited the machine after the final rinse section, it was washed clean, shining, and bone dry.

It still amazes me today that operators insist on using the flat basket technique which means spoons collecting water, longer drying times, and usually the cutlery having to be rewashed. It's a waste of time, chemicals, and energy, which ultimately means a waste of money.

It's worth mentioning that some chefs' knives are not suitable for washing through a commercial dishwasher. The combination of the chemicals and high temperatures can be damaging to steel blades and handles. These need to be carefully hand washed.

Glass basket

Glasswasher baskets vary in size from 500mm² for large glasswashers, 400mm² (and 450mm² which is less common) for medium glasswashers, and 350mm² baskets for small cabinet glasswashers. The sides of these baskets are higher than that for dishes to prevent glasses from falling over.

Glass baskets can be completely flat and open or have a slight incline which helps the water run off the bottom of the glasses. You can buy glass baskets that have separators built in that prevent the glasses from hitting together while the wash cycle is in full motion. These separators are effective when you are washing delicate stemware or expensive glasses that need protection. Make sure that your staff are placing cups and glasses upside down inside the glass baskets, otherwise they'll just fill with wash and rinse water and will not get cleaned or dried.

Water treatment

The quality of the fresh water that feeds into your dishwasher and glasswasher has a large bearing on the results that you seek and on the lifespan of your machines. Throughout the UK, the water hardness varies quite dramatically from one region to the next. This means that hard water has a greater concentration of minerals such as calcium and magnesium than softer water.

Hard water is safe for humans to drink, although when left untreated in appliances such as your dishwasher, it causes limescale build-up. If you have hard water, you may notice that the inside of your machine has a white or rusty brown residue coating the inside of it. This also builds up in the unseen parts of your machine where it can cause damage to internal pipes, boilers, and elements.

According to a study carried out by The Carbon Trust, even a 1 mm build-up of limescale on a heating element will increase its energy demand by 7%.[5] This has a direct result on the efficiency of the element and on how long it will last under these conditions, leading to engineer visits and early replacement of parts. In areas of the country where the water is hard, the results of your dishes and glasses will not be great. They will be clean but may appear dull and cloudy.

If in doubt, have your water tested for hardness. It's a simple strip test that you can carry out yourself or ask your dishwasher company to test it for you. What can be done to combat hard water? At this point, it is worth speaking about water softeners and other water treatment systems like reverse osmosis (RO).

---

5   Carbon Trust, 'Low Temperature Hot Water Boilers', www.carbon-trust.com

Water softener

A water softener is used in areas where the water is hard enough to have a negative effect on a commercial dishwasher. It is a device either placed externally or built into the machine. Built-in softeners are automatic, and external water softeners can be manual or automatic. Adding a water softener to your dishwasher will cost more money initially and a small ongoing payment for softener salt, but the benefit for getting more from your machine far outweighs these costs.

Water softeners, whether external or integral, sit between the water inlet feed to the dishwasher and the internal components of the machine, thus ensuring that the water is soft. Both types must be regularly topped up with salt and the frequency of this depends upon the hardness of the local water and the capacity of the water softener itself. The manufacturer's guide or your dishwashing company will help you get this right.

The softener trades the calcium and magnesium in the hard water for the sodium in the salt and an ion exchange happens. To ensure that the water softener correctly does its job, it must be regenerated from time to time. With a manual softener this regeneration is done manually and with an automatic softener (you've guessed it), regeneration happens automatically as set by the manufacturer or the installer.

The salt used in a water softener varies in appearance, although the best kind for your dishwasher is in the form of pellets, followed by granular type salt. The larger pellets have a lot of space between them which allows for the water to flow better. Do not use table salt.

Reverse osmosis (RO)

A reverse osmosis system is slightly different from a water softener in that it uses a very fine filter system or membrane to get rid of impurities in the water before it reaches the internal components of your dishwasher or glasswasher.

They have been heralded in recent years as the best way to get pure water into your machine to ensure quality results and to prolong the lifespan of your appliance.

There are arguments for and against using reverse osmosis. The initial cost of having one is high and the running costs can increase your water bill significantly. In some instances, the water used to produce 1 litre of pure water can be as high a ratio as 4:1. In fine dining restaurants with high standards, or units that have a large volume of glasses and stemware which requires labour intensive hand polishing, then a reverse osmosis unit is beneficial.

If you think you could benefit from having a RO unit, do your research. The cost and amount of water used varies between dishwasher manufacturers and specialist water treatment companies. In general, a water softener does the job. A RO unit is the most appropriate addition if perfect glassware is required. Remember that these water treatment units themselves require occasional servicing in order to run at optimum performance.

Grease traps

It's not just the water flowing into a dishwasher which must be considered. The effluent discharge or drain water is also worthy of note. Fats, oils, and grease (FOG) which don't bind with the detergents in either the sinks or the dishwasher end up flowing down into the drainage system.

As the wastewater cools further down the drainage pipes, this FOG starts to solidify and build up and creates blockages in the system. This can cause the restaurateur costly problems. When allowed to travel down into the main sewerage network, they accumulate into massive lumps which cost the taxpayers hundreds of thousands of pounds a year for the local councils to manage. These 'Fat Bergs' are a combination of household waste and commercial kitchen waste.

One way to manage the discharged wastewater in a commercial kitchen is to install a grease trap underneath or at the end of the line so that it catches the wastewater from the end of the dishwashing system. Do not place it directly after the dishwasher, make sure that it catches the sink water too. There are automatic clean and manual grease traps available. They are not all the same so do your research along with your dishwashing company or a water treatment specialist and work out the size and type that would benefit your setup.

4

Can't I Just Use A Domestic Dishwasher?

A domestic dishwasher is different from a commercial dishwasher. Although the principles of wash, rinse, and drain are the same, there are things that separate them. The main difference between the two appliances is that a domestic dishwasher takes longer to complete a cycle, and if used more than a few times a day it falls behind a commercial machine.

A typical commercial machine takes two to three minutes to wash, rinse, and dry a basket of dishes. For a domestic dishwashing machine to complete the equivalent process it can take anywhere between forty-five minutes to an hour and a half. In a working restaurant this would immediately prove to be an impossible situation.

The workload that a commercial machine can handle is massive in comparison, and the price of each demonstrates this well. A commercial dishwasher will cost anything from around £1500 + VAT (Value Added Tax) upwards, whereas a decent domestic machine is £400 including VAT. Domestic dishwashers are now part of our 'throw away' culture. Many people do not get their domestic machines repaired anymore. If it's an expensive part that needs to be replaced, most householders will buy a new machine.

Domestic machines are typically a combination of plastic and painted ferrous metal, which doesn't suit such a harsh environment. The robust stainless-steel body of a commercial machine is designed to handle the day-to-day mayhem that can be the norm in a professional kitchen. It is less of a throw away culture in the commercial side as usually the initial price has been such a large outlay and so professional kitchens and bars will look to get their machine repaired and not replaced.

Hand washing dishes versus a commercial dishwasher

When it comes to installing a new commercial dishwasher into premises that have never had one before, the feel-good factor is enormous. The overall impact that it has on a kitchen is massive, as many areas will increase in efficiency. Staff morale is given an injection. If they were not appreciated before, whoever made the decision to buy the commercial machine will hear a collective sigh of relief. When a new machine is put in place, the staff can see the immediate impact that it has on their daily routine. Of course, there is a degree of change involved and a learning curve, but once they get used to it there is no going back to hand washing.

Other positives of a commercial dishwasher over hand washing include:

Time

Apart from controlling the bacteria that can poison us, time is perhaps the greatest gift that a commercial dishwasher gives to a busy kitchen. Instead of thirty minutes to wash and dry fifty plates, a medium cycle of a dishwasher is around two minutes and thirty seconds. Each 500mm² plate basket holds eighteen dinner plates, so three basket loads take care of that volume with some spare capacity.

If the machine is working correctly and the rinse aid is good, dishes will be washed and dried within ten minutes. This is time that staff can be doing something else, or if it's at the end of a shift, they can go home on time.

Manpower

A commercial machine can do more than one person. If previously you had a few people doing the dishes, eg one washing and one drying, you can now deploy a member of the dishwashing staff to another area of the kitchen or restaurant to carry out work.

Cost of labour

If time is being saved at the end of a shift with dishes now going through a commercial dishwasher, then you won't have to pay overtime for staff not being able to finish on time. Also, you may not need as many dishwashing staff on your books.

Energy used

The physical energy output of your staff is not as great with a commercial dishwasher and they will thank you for it. Where your hot water and boiler are concerned, constantly topping up wash water and rinse water in open sinks with near boiling water uses up a great deal of energy. This will cost you a fortune over the years.

Breakages

When staff are careful with how they load a machine basket then there are far less breakages than hand washing. After all, this is what led to the invention of the first dishwasher! Breakages are especially prevalent when hand washing dirty glasses. Many restaurant bars do not have two sinks, and if so, they are normally small for space-saving purposes. This adds in the danger of staff cutting themselves on broken glass and broken crockery and is over and above the costs involved in constant replacements.

Temperatures for sanitising

Even if you have a second sink full of very hot water for rinsing the dishes, it will quickly lose temperature. Most machines have a built-in rinse control device or rinse thermostop which extends the wash cycle to ensure that the machine rinses at 82°C (for environmental health purposes). Hand washing cannot cope with these high temperatures, even if your staff are wearing a decent pair of rubber gloves.

Strength of chemicals

Machine dishwashing detergent should never be used for hand washing dishes as it is too strong and often contains highly alkaline caustic (sodium hydroxide). Constant hand washing in milder detergent is not good for human skin either and can cause skin conditions to develop. Therefore, if your staff are hand washing plates, they should wear gloves.

The downside of wearing gloves is that staff cannot feel the plates as they clean them to make sure that the debris has been properly washed off. Only careful inspection of every plate will ensure that they are clean.

Staff health

As well as skin conditions being a problem, if staff spend hours every day bent over a sink, it will take its toll because of the constant stooping posture. If your KPs are tall, then several hours of bending over the sink every day will lead to long-term lower back problems. Keeping your staff healthy at work should be a top priority.

Hygiene

A consistently high level of hygiene is imperative in a commercial establishment. Each dish and piece of cutlery must be washed to a high standard and then sanitised at a high temperature of 82°C, above the survival temperature for harmful bacteria to thrive.

Cutlery polishing

A separate cutlery polishing machine can be bought for this function, and many busy kitchens have a machine separate from their dishwasher that carries this out. However, you will no doubt have a chemical supplier that you already work with. If they are good at what they do, then they will work with your dishwasher to get the concentration levels correct so that your cutlery is coming out of the machine clean and with no need for further polishing.

CASE STUDY: NICOLA IRVING, HEAD CHEF AT THE LOCHSIDE HOUSE HOTEL

Nicola has been in the hospitality industry for twenty-seven years and worked her way up through the ranks. She has been the head chef in The Lochside for over seventeen years. She attributes the success of her kitchen to her staff and having good systems in place that work well.

How many covers do you do at your busiest time?

Nicola: *We do roughly 700 covers over the course of one day.*

In your experience does having a good dishwashing system create benefits in the kitchen, or is there a difference if it is a bad system?

Nicola: *Firstly, having a dishwasher is the best thing ever. If you don't have a dishwasher it is like having your left arm broken. For profits we have a Manning Guide that we work to within the company, and when your dishwasher is not working then your manning power doubles or trebles so having no dishwasher you can sometimes be three times your price, so profit wise yes you do save money in the long run having a good dishwasher, but manning time can treble when you are without one.*

Manning time being bringing a kitchen porter (KP) in?

Nicola: *Three. Three KPs are the equivalent to one machine. Three need to be brought in if your one machine is down as you are having to hand wash the dishes, and this also depends on how big your functions are as well.*

Did you call that a Manning Cost?

Nicola: Yes, it's a Manning Cost. We work to a budget. Our kitchen budget is 18% in a week, we normally sit roughly at 14%, with weddings on its 12% at the highest peak. If your dishwasher breaks down your budget can creep back up to 16 or 18% because you are pulling more staff in to do the one job that your main machine would do for you. Sometimes you might have two dishwashing machines down so you need four people in to do the equivalent work that the two machines would normally do.

So that affects the cost of the meals and affects other costs?

Nicola: It affects everything, it's very labour intensive. Honestly, a dishwasher saves time and money in the business.

If you were setting up a new dishwashing system, would you do this yourselves or would you get someone in to help and advise you?

Nicola: We would definitely get a company in and we would probably look at a bigger machine because the ones we have in are fantastic but in this type of business we are continuously growing. Sometimes two or three machines are not enough so you can imagine the figures and numbers we do – there is a lot of prep work. We have a great deal of tubs, trays, bowls, etc to be cleaned prior to having people in the restaurant.

When you start refurbishment, you are going to go from 700 covers a day to how many?

Nicola: It could be anything, you could have 500 covers between two functions, you could have a birthday party on and 400 covers in your restaurant. You are looking at between 700 and 1000 covers, and that will just depend on what functions, weddings, and other events are on within the hotel on a particular day.

In your opinion would it be better to have one big machine that would take care of all of that or one medium-sized machine and another passthrough, so if anything goes wrong with the main machine you at least have a backup?

Nicola: *I would always say it is better to have a backup. I had three machines and I took one out of the back kitchen to put in a salad prep area and I believe it was one of the worst decisions I've made. One of the most stupid mistakes I've done in my life! On the off chance that the two dishwashers break down in the kitchen, and this has happened in the past, then we have no machine for back up. 100%, I would recommend having a backup machine.*

With so much experience, why would you bring someone else in to have a look at how you would design the dishwashing systems?

Nicola: *Everything in technology moves forward so fast, as with dishwashers, computers, etc so I would probably leave it to the people who know best, with their advice and what to use nowadays. I'm stuck in a kitchen and don't get to see the advances in the machinery. I would bring in the people with the expertise in that area to recommend the correct system for us. It's better to have people that know what they're talking about, rather than me buying what I think I would like.*

So you would prefer to have someone in with the expertise in that area and work with you, taking in your opinions and the plans that you have and advise accordingly?

Nicola: Yes, 100%.

What three things as well as the dishwashing system in the kitchen keep you awake at night?

Nicola: Staff, and sometimes deliveries not arriving, or maybe they don't have a certain product in. For instance, two weeks ago the Fruit Market in Scotland (Glasgow) I buy from burned down, and I got a phone call at 3.45 am to tell me that all the veg that I'd ordered wasn't available. I could get the basics like carrots and broccoli but specifics that I'd been looking for like turned vegetables and prepped veg that a company at the market does for me wouldn't be arriving. So, I had to look for alternatives, and there is always an alternative. If the dishwasher breaks down, the alternative is we have to fill the sinks, get someone else in and wash the dishes by hand!

Staff can be a major worry. Machines are your biggest worry. If your machines break down, and that's any machine in the kitchen, then there are problems. Your dishwasher is your biggest machine, and I'm not going to lie. If an ice machine breaks down then we can buy bags of ice, if a blender breaks down, we can crush food with other tools, but if your dishwasher breaks down then you've got to wash then by hand. Nightmare!

I would say, your machines, your staff, and deliveries cause the biggest problems. Whether they are late, or they don't come, or you're expecting someone in to make a repair and they take five days to appear. It depends on what company you are dealing with, and most people are professional.

What part do KPs play in your kitchen running smoothly?

Nicola: At the end of the day if you don't have kitchen porters available, your hotel does not run. It's that serious.

If you have nobody there to wash your dishes then you don't have clean plates to serve your next customer, so I believe a kitchen porter is every bit as important in the hotel as a general manager, a manager, or head chef. We all have important roles to play and a kitchen porter, please believe me, is probably the main person through there. They keep your production line going because if you have no clean plates then you can't feed your customers. So, without them, you are totally lost.

What is the main difference between having a good KP and a bad KP?

Nicola: *Cleanliness and time! You get lazy people, and you get good hard-working people. A lot of people do not want to work for minimum wage. It is nice to have someone come in that works hard and we have mutual respect for one another. It's great when they are willing to learn. It's also about how you treat people, as to how they reward you back.*

With regards to the dishwashing systems, is there anything else that you think is valuable for us to know?

Nicola: *Because I've done this for such a long time, I remember before dishwashers we had to fill one sink up with hot water and bubbles and the other one with cold water. We then had to wash and rinse every single item by hand which would take about five hours, whereas it would have taken a dishwasher twenty minutes to do the lot. Looking back from now to twenty odd years ago, I think, 'How did we survive without a dishwasher?' It's like the mobile phone. I look at youngsters now and think that they don't know any different. Technology moves on all the time; I mean if we didn't have a dishwasher in our kitchen our guys would be completely lost.*

Also, for legal reasons like environmental health, it is great that the dishwashers have buttons on them telling you what the temperature is and rinsing guides, whereas before it was just hot wash and cold rinse, so you did not know what the water temperature was. We now have data and information that we can collect, and this helps us with the running of the kitchen.

Nicola Irving, Head Chef at The Lochside House Hotel, Restaurant, Lodges & Spa in New Cumnock, Ayrshire

---

The story so far

As can be seen, there is a strong case for having a commercial dishwasher and these are over and above the environmental health requirements. When all of the preceding information is taken into account and carefully considered, it's easy to see that if you are missing even one of these factors, or if there are inefficiencies, then this will have a significant impact on your running costs and the profit that your restaurant will realise come year end.

In Part Two we look further into your current setup and examine how you organise and run your premises. This will help you understand that there is a more holistic approach that you must adopt for success, although looking at the details will make all the difference.

PART TWO
LOOK AROUND TO LOOK FORWARD

5
Your New Wash Area

How do you currently run your restaurant and kitchen? Does it run like a Swiss watch even when you are not there? Can you take a few weeks off on holiday and not worry about how it is performing because you know the staff will execute every detail to a high standard and take pride in doing so?

If you can relax when you're not there because you have efficient systems in place, then well done. Read on though because you will find tweaks that you can make to streamline your operation further.

If not, then read on, as the rest of the book concentrates on looking at how your place is running now, what to look out for, how to help fix the problems, and how to avoid them happening in the future. This will help you move towards working on your business rather than working in it. First, let's have a look at your operation from a different perspective.

Keep it clean

As a business owner in the restaurant industry your reputation is vital to your success. How your customers perceive your overall image can go a long way in enhancing or damaging that reputation. When you own a restaurant, it is important to acknowledge that everyone you encounter is a potential customer. Picture how hard you work to keep your restaurant, the kitchen, and the toilets clean and working like clockwork. However, one area often neglected is the space under or around the commercial dishwasher or glasswasher.

I have years of experience going into pubs, hotels, restaurants, and cafés where everywhere is spotless, except the area round the commercial ware washer. Granted this area can be hard to reach, but it is possible. Dishwasher service engineers endure dirty situations in which to carry out their work and this is part and parcel of doing the job. In some extreme circumstances though, it can be extremely unhygienic. Environmental health and a health and safety officer would not be comfortable if they were aware of some of the environments.

Now consider one of your best customers walking into your restaurant kitchen and looking in and around your commercial dishwasher. What would they see? What would they think? Would this impact their view of your establishment in a positive or negative way? These questions are worth thinking about. It is also worth bearing in mind that your service engineers are potential customers too.

I recommend making sure that cleaning in and around the dishwasher is part of your staff's daily or weekly routine. If you have a corner passthrough dishwasher that is hard to get out, then you could request that as part of a maintenance contract, that your dishwasher engineer pulls the machine out safely and lets the staff clean behind it. Even if this is only every six months, it is far better than every six years when the machine is being replaced.

It's refreshing to hear the request, 'Can you let us clean in there while you have the machine out?' – but this doesn't always happen. If they don't offer, I suggest to the staff that they have an opportunity to clean behind the machine while it is out of its normal position. Whether you build it into your own routine or through a maintenance contract, it is wise not to neglect this area.

Where do your high standards end?

The culture that runs throughout your restaurant is extremely important. It must be one of respect and high standards, because like it or not, your customers will sense how good or bad your staff culture is, as it inevitably filters through to them during service. Your staff should treat each other and everyone that comes through your doors (including the service and delivery doors) as they would treat your good customers.

As we are all aware, everyone has an opinion these days and to voice it to the whole world takes only a few clicks or finger taps. Let me give you an example where in my opinion, the balance of respect was way off the perceived ambience of the restaurant.

I called a customer to arrange a site visit. I had a wonderful experience when researching the establishment and when talking with the general manager on the phone. The place already felt like a 5-star restaurant and that was before I had even stepped a foot inside of it. I arrived at the scheduled date and time and entered through the back kitchen door, or as it's commonly known, the tradesman's entrance. It was just before a heavy lunch service and I wanted to observe how both the dishwasher and the KPs performed when they were at their busiest and under pressure. You get a real taste for things at this time of the day. As I was going through the motions, I couldn't help but overhear one of the older chefs screaming profanities at one of the junior chefs, bringing him down in front of everyone. The young guy was visibly shaken, but everyone else got on with what they were doing. It seemed that this behaviour had sadly become acceptable and normalised in this kitchen. This immediately changed my perception of the place. I wondered if the restaurant owner knew and if this was part of the culture that came from the top?

Is your place like that? Has the way that some of the celebrity chefs behave towards their colleagues become so commonplace that it's cool to bully them? It makes for good television but in real life, it doesn't usually sit well with the casual observer, and that could be the dishwasher engineer or a sales rep. Remember that dishwasher service engineers are customers too. Most likely they have a family and friends that they speak to about their experiences on the job.

It's nice to be nice

When your service engineer comes to start a job, do you or your staff offer them a tea or a coffee, or a cold drink? There are mixed views on this subject. Some people are of the opinion that the engineer is there to do a job. It is costing you money and they are getting paid for carrying out the job. Therefore, they do not need to benefit from a free drink from your establishment. They let the engineer get on with the job and it doesn't cross their mind to offer them anything.

Then there is another school of thought. These people are naturally inclined to offer any tradesperson a tea or a coffee anyway, because they are doing a job for you and ultimately helping you out.

From a tradesman's point of view, it is always nicer to be offered a refreshment when on the job. It shows that you care about them, and it also (probably subliminally) will make them care more about you and your dishwashing machine. There is evidence that shows that a small gift like this creates a subconscious obligation and it will probably lead to a better outcome for you:

'The general rule says that a person who acts in a certain way towards us is entitled to a similar return action.'[6] In other words, your engineer will work harder or longer to find the right solution for the repair of your dishwasher if they have been treated with respect and maybe even offered a coffee.

I know customers that offer the engineer something to eat whenever they are out and the engineer is well looked after. Ultimately though, it's just nice. I still make an offer of tea or coffee after greeting a service engineer into my home, because I know that it works on me.

---

6   Robert B Cialdini, PhD (1984) *Influence: The psychology of persuasion.* New York: William Morrow and Company.

Make your restaurant a positive place

Your staff are your greatest assets and when they work in harmony with your vision, anything is possible. When they can see what you want to achieve in your restaurant and they know their value and contribution is appreciated, good staff will help you reach your goals.

Restaurants are well-known for their high turnover of staff and as a restaurant owner or head chef, this can be an ongoing problem that is difficult to resolve. Even if you know that a potential member of staff has long-term plans to move off elsewhere, it may be of value to have them work with you if their attitude and ethics match your own. As Joy Zarine states in her book *The Five Star Formula*, 'I assure you, a great employee for six months is better than an average one for three years.'[7]

Getting the right team in place is not easy. Choose wisely. Hire slowly and fire fast. This should be applied to all staff from the front of house to the back of the kitchen. Whether your customers see them or not, they will feel the vibe the staff create in your restaurant's atmosphere. Ness Sekakmia, the General Manager at The Oatlands Park Hotel in Weybridge sums it up nicely: 'Happy staff, happy guests'.

---

7   Joy Zarine (2017) *The Five Star Formula*. Gorleston: Rethink Press.

To get the most out of your commercial dishwashing and glasswashing machines and properly sweat these assets, your staff play a crucial part. They have to be good guys (like you) and they have to be willing to learn on an ongoing basis. They need to be well versed and properly educated in how to work and take care of your dishwasher and glasswasher.

CASE STUDY: DAVID ALLISON, HEAD CHEF AT THE INN ON THE LOCH RESTAURANT

David has been a chef for over twenty years. He has been at the Inn for twelve years and has held the role of head chef for ten years. David points out that the culture within his team is paramount to building a successful restaurant business.

You have a great atmosphere in your kitchen. How have you created that and how do you maintain it during prolonged busy periods?

David: The job is hard enough without being able to have a laugh; we have a laugh a lot in the kitchen. There's a bit of give and take with the guys, you can't be hard on them all of the time. Some chefs will not take a bit of joking from another chef because they think that they're higher up the ranks than them. I just try and be fair with my guys and I think it works because I try to be firm but fair.

If we can't get on together then it's not going to be much fun to work together. We are like a family here as we work long hours, so we need to get on. There is an element of banter and we have a great laugh, but we do all get our heads down and get back into chef mode when it is busy to get the job done.

Do you hire on skill or personality?

David: *Both help. A lot of chefs come in with skill, some have been a* chef de partie *for years but don't fit into the grand scheme of things. The quality may not be as good as you would expect from a chef of that level and sometimes it's the attitude. Do they fit in with the other guys? Are they rubbing them up the wrong way? Unfortunately, some people don't connect with certain people. It's trying to whittle out the right people for the job and over time it works, you can see who's fitting in to the team, who's a team player, or who is a freeloader. The right person will fit in with us.*

It's trial and error and if we find the right person they tend to stay. It's also hard as people don't come out of their shell straight away, so everyone coming into the business gets a three-month trial to make sure their skills and personality fit in. They have to be adaptable. Very important to find the right people that you can depend on.

Some people fit straight in; they are the easy ones. You can work with them; you can work on the job and properly train them how to do it.

Some chefs we've tried in the past are stuck in their ways. They're not willing to move or learn anymore. You have to be adaptable and you adapt to every team member that you have in with you too. There are certain laughs you'll have with one, there's others that you know where the line is with them. You have a working relationship and you have a friendship. There is a bond in the kitchen.

When a team member is off sick, we will come in and cover each other's shift, because we know how hard it is with someone not there. We have each other's back and I think this is where part of that strong bond comes from.

How important to you is staff wellbeing and satisfaction at work, provided of course that the work still gets done?

David: It's essential. If you look after your staff and you're good to them they will want to come in and dedicate their life and time to the job. I sell the vision of what we're doing and where we're going for the owners, to my staff, and we all go for it. Looking after your staff and making sure they are well paid keeps the morale in the kitchen going, and it makes them want to come to work. We all have off days though and if you show that you care about each member then they will put it back into the business, and they give it their all.

Having that general friendship with them and still being a boss helps as well. It's a balancing act and it has taken me years to perfect. It is hard and only through time you learn. In my first job as a chef I think the power went to my head and I demanded respect rather than gaining respect and over time you realise through loosing staff, that this approach just doesn't work.

You have to help your staff grow. This permeates through the business. Our front of house team is fantastic, we've all got such a good friendship with front of house and the customers pick up on this, and our customers love them.

If you don't have good front of house staff the atmosphere is just terrible and the whole experience is just bad. It's good to understand people and you definitely need that in a business.

This does help the business. Although we are selling food, we have to sell a standard of food, but we also need a certain standard of service as well. That's what our job is all about.

If you don't have a good front of house, then the ambience can be bad. I've been in a few places where the front of house staff are terrible and there is no atmosphere. When the food comes out it's mediocre and I think it sets up the whole thing. You think to yourself – 'what am I doing here?'.

It sets up the whole meal experience. If you've got that all in place and everybody is happy, the staff are happy, then the customer sees that.

In my kitchen I can tell when a chef is down, when there's something wrong with them because their standard of food drops. It's the little things you learn working with people all these years. You become more of a social worker in the kitchen than a chef! It's understanding people and being able to read them.

We need this to offer a complete service, and staff satisfaction and wellbeing are definitely high up in our priorities as a company.

David Allison, Head Chef at The Inn on the Loch Restaurant in Lanark, South Lanarkshire

6
Finding The Best Machine

When these machines are not understood and go unloved, the staff will be the first to complain about how bad the machinery is and how you should go out and buy a new one. If I had a pound for every time I was asked, 'Can you just tell them you can't fix it so that they have to buy us a new one?', then I would have a good bit of money set aside to buy a commercial dishwasher for my own house. Typically, this happens when machines are bought below the specifications that they should have been and are not fit for purpose from day one. They struggle and the staff know that it just can't cope with the daily toil they are putting it through.

However, space, budget, and timing are all relevant to each restaurant setting. Although this book is aimed to help restaurant owners and chefs, it is equally applicable to other areas of the catering and hospitality industry and is definitely relevant to hotels, cafés and bistros, coffee shops, pubs, social clubs, staff working in schools and hospital canteens, garden centres, churches, and anywhere else that needs or could benefit from a commercial dishwasher.

It may be the case that, regardless of the establishment that you own or work in, the local Environmental Health Officer (EHO) has paid a visit and requested that a commercial dishwasher be installed or your existing one renewed. If this is the case, then please keep reading. This book will help you acquire the best machine for your budget and arm you with tips and tricks to ultimately make life easier.

It won't matter what make your existing machines are because there are universal rules that apply to most machines on the market. Insert these rules into your other kitchen and bar systems and pass them onto key members of staff so that they will know the simple check list of steps to go through on a daily basis. Soon enough, these rules will be adopted, and you may notice that you are seeing your dishwasher service engineer less.

Dishwash systems are expensive (buy cheap, buy twice)

Commercial dishwashers are brilliant pieces of kit and are vital to a commercial kitchen in a restaurant.

The staff cannot be without one. They are the most complicated piece of machinery in the kitchen with so many moving mechanical parts and electronic components, however, they have parts in them that can fail over time or fail through misuse. When a dishwasher breaks down, the nightmare begins.

Let's look at a following timeline of what can result when a dishwasher has broken down or has been failing for a long time... Imagine your dishwashing machine breaks down and, as service progresses, a backlog of dirty plates and dishes starts to build up. Chefs are waiting for the correct plates and frustrations build as the food is ready but can't be plated up. This results in long waiting times between courses and angry customers. Over time, regular customers notice the change in restaurant culture as internal frustrations begin to spill over and staff quit and leave for somewhere with better facilities. Customer complaints and bad reviews on social media and online start to rise or customers simply won't return. As a result, cash turnover drops, takings are down, remaining staff get less in tips, and you (as the owner) are seen as a penny pincher. Staff morale lowers as strangers get drafted in to cover absent staff and vacancies. More money is spent on marketing and advertising. Wages and staff are cut to meet ongoing costs and standards slip to an all-time low. After repeated visits, environmental health comes in and closes your restaurant.

Obviously, this is the worst-case scenario but it does happen. If your Environmental Health Officer has seen and noted on multiple visits that you have consistently neglected the state of your dishwasher and surrounds, then they may close down your kitchen, without which your restaurant is only an empty hall with tables and chairs.

Your dishwasher does not need to fail completely for it to cause problems. A customer's perception of your establishment can be drawn in a negative way just because of one simple thing. Let's look at the result of when a dishwasher or glasswasher isn't doing its job properly.

As mentioned earlier, lipstick on a glass can be a real put off for some customers. Lipstick is a tough one for glasswashers. Global cosmetics manufacturers pride themselves in declaring how their lipstick will last all night and that it does not need reapplication. Lipstick that does come off the lips onto glasses can be difficult to remove. A good working machine that is properly drawing in quality chemicals should do the job.

I stayed the night in London and attended a conference in another hotel the next day. I was there for business and the value from the conference was excellent. The facilities were good, and the staff couldn't have been nicer. There were bottles of water on each table and glasses to drink out of. A few of the glasses had lip imprints around the rim that hadn't been removed. I avoided those glasses and it immediately got me thinking that I was glad that I hadn't spent the previous night there. I had to remind myself that it wasn't that big a deal. However, the reality is that I'm not alone in thinking this way.

As a business owner you will realise that customers can be fickle. Attention to detail is important and if you aren't paying attention and you don't have staff and an infrastructure that you can trust, then what results will you achieve?

The unsung heroes: no one cares until there is a problem

We all know how peaceful it is to watch a swan effortlessly gliding across the surface of a still pond. Underneath the water though is where the hard work takes place. This is a great analogy when it comes to your dishwasher. Your dishwasher may or may not look like a great piece of kit. I suppose they can be closer to the ugly duckling of the kitchen, but how it performs is its main asset. Under the shiny stainless-steel exterior is a myriad of working parts that have been engineered to work hard together to get you the results that you desire – clean dishes, cutlery, cups and glasses, first time, every time.

We liken the commercial dishwasher to a car. A dishwasher washes your dishes, a car can drive you from A to B. You can spend as little or as much as you like on either, buy new or used (reconditioned), buy an expensive model, a middle of the road model, or buy the cheapest of the cheap. You get what you pay for and every time you put your dishwasher through a cycle, it's like mileage building up on your car. This is a good way to look at an older machine that is now breaking down. You can spend money to bring it back up to a decent standard, but something else may fail in a few months. If your car is ten years old and it starts to give you costly problems, what would you do? Keep throwing money at it or trade it in for a newer model? Usually it's the latter.

When your dishwasher starts to develop problems, staff realise just how much they need it working properly. Sometimes it is only when it breaks down that they really appreciate how tough the job is without a working machine. Wear and tear is normal for any working dishwasher or glasswasher. However, most of the time it's how staff treat the machines that can cause problems.

Mistakes your staff are making right now

Your staff are on the frontline with your dishwasher and how they operate, clean, and treat it will have a direct result on how this machine performs. This chapter highlights the mistakes that your staff may be making right now.

If you can get a basic understanding of these mistakes, get your staff to stop making them, and train on ways to prevent them from happening, then this will save you a serious amount of money in engineer call outs, labour, and dishwasher parts. Sorting these mistakes out can add years onto the lifespan of your machine.

1. Do not put cutlery in basket racks meant for plates or cups. The cutlery, especially small spoons, fall through the holes in these baskets. A teaspoon burning out a wash pump can cost over £1000. Cutlery, wooden spoons, and spatulas hanging through the bottom of a basket will stop the bottom wash and rinse arms from spinning and properly performing their duties. Use specialist cutlery baskets that have a finer mesh or stack the cutlery in a cutlery basket. That way the wash water gets to each piece evenly and the rinse water can dispel off them for quicker drying.

2. Do not place basket racks on top of the glasswasher or dishwasher. Staff may struggle with space for somewhere to put the basket, but the top of the machine is not the place. Water ingress in the form of either slops from dirty glasses or dripping water from clean glasses will cause problems. If this doesn't seep in and affect the electronics of the machine costing you hundreds of pounds in damage, then it will serve to bind the top panel to the machine and stick them together like glue. This can add on significant time to a job when your dishwasher

service engineer needs to remove this panel for a repair or service. If you really are stuck for space to use, buy a purpose-built drip tray for the job. They are inexpensive and effective. Problem solved.

3. The top of a passthrough dishwasher is not for storage. When large items are placed on top of the hood of a passthrough dishwasher, it creates an imbalance between the stainless-steel hood and the hood springs at the back of the machine. This places unnecessary stress on the springs and shortens their lifespan. When hood springs snap it is difficult to lift the hood, and it will no longer stay in the open position by itself until a tricky repair is made. It is also a health and safety issue as the heavy hood becomes a risk as it's always wanting to close. Drying tea towels and cloths on top of the hood is also a bad idea. These tend to fall down the back of the machine on top of important components, which over time can heat up and become a fire hazard.

4. Not properly scraping plates is a bad habit that leads to food, sugar sachets, and butter wrappers going into the machine, clogging up the filters, and dirtying the water more than it should. If these get through the filters and make their way into the wash pump and wash system, they will clog up the wash arms and the machine. This can result in costly repairs.

5. The wash and rinse arm manifolds need to be removed from the machine and cleaned. Many people neglect to do this. When these get clogged up, they can no longer spin properly, especially if they are clogged up in the middle at the manifold. When they don't move or spin properly, they won't clean. Sometimes it results in jets of water being sprayed out of the sides of the door and creating a pool of water at the front of your machine. When it comes to glasswashers, they seem to collect fluff and hair. Make sure that this is cleaned out. Be careful of small pieces of broken glass that may be lodged in the wash manifolds. Use blue roll or an old cloth to wipe these down and use the torch from your mobile phone to see.

6. Not cleaning out the wash arm jets regularly will result in unclean dishes. The wash water has to pass through the wash jets with enough pressure to spin the wash arms to ensure an even wash of the dishes.

7. Clean out the rinse arm jets. If it is the rinse arms that are clogged up, then this is usually a sign of a serious problem. Have staff clean them out but report it if it happens regularly. It may be that the manifold is split, and the wash and rinse water is mixing, or the rinse boost pump impellor is starting to break up and work its way around the rinse system. You will need a repair carried out by a service engineer.

8. Even seasoned staff can fail to realise that there are top wash and rinse arms. If no one knows they are there, then they can get clogged up and neglected. Sometimes they remain like that for years and staff just live with the fact that the dishes are not that clean. This is common in restaurants that have a high turnover of staff.

9. Check that chemical bottles have enough in them. When the chemical bottles run empty, the pumps will draw air. If you have an external dosing unit and staff know how to prime the chemicals back up, then that's not too bad. However, by the time the staff realise that the dishes or glasses are not clean it is too late. It will take at least several washes to get the new chemicals primed back into the machine again. Depending on the machine you have, you may be able to press programme buttons on the machine to prime up the chemicals, but if not then this may mean that it's the same basket of dishes going through the machine until they are clean, or dishes being put back out while still dirty.

10. Chemicals in the wrong bottles is a mistake. Detergent tubing in the rinse aid bottle and rinse aid tubing in the detergent bottle can leave a cloudy film on glasses and a detergent residue on plates as caustic is now being fed through the rinse. If left unchecked the detergent will damage the internal rinse system, especially the

boiler element. In a glasswasher, pints of beer or lager will not be able to hold a head when poured.

11. Do not pour rinse aid into the wash tank of the machine when the pump is not working. The rinse aid pump injects rinse aid into the boiler system for the final rinse at the end of the cycle. This cannot be done manually. If staff pour the rinse aid into the wash tank like they may detergent, then they are as well as pouring it down the drain – it is a waste of money.

12. If the wash basket is overloaded, dishes can't be reached properly by the wash and rinse jets and remain dirty. Staff will have to rewash the dishes.

13. Underloading the wash basket is a waste of water, energy, and chemicals and staff are better to keep the half empty basket until there are more dishes before putting the machine through a cycle.

14. Pushing the glass basket in too quickly may cause the glasses to break. You see this often in busy bars where the staff are running around and are pressed for time between serving customers.

15. Slamming the door or hood down results in door hinges breaking, door catches being worn quickly, and door magnets breaking off. Sometimes passthrough hoods become split, and splash guards are broken off. Wash water can

escape onto the floor and it's expensive to fix these issues.

16. Check that glasses are empty before putting them into the glasswasher. It can be difficult for staff to see everything in a glass when they are working under pressure and the lighting may not be great behind your bar. However, try and instil it into them to look carefully for chewing gum, confetti, etc as these can clog up the wash system, cost money on engineer call outs and labour, and occasionally burn out the wash pump motor.

17. Tipping beer slops into the glasswasher makes the wash water dirtier than it should be, and it has a neutralising effect on the glasswash detergent. It dilutes it down and renders the chemical practically ineffective. Have staff pour excess drink down a sink or into a bucket for disposing of later.

18. Do not remove filters before draining machine down. When the filters are removed this means that the drain is the first and final line of defence for trapping food scraps etc, when the machine drains down. This leads to blocked drains and blocked drain pumps. If the drain pump burns out, then this is a costly mistake.

19. Do not wash with the same wash water all day. It is good practice to empty down your machine, give the filters a clean, wipe it down and restart

it with fresh water after every service. If your restaurant does a breakfast service, a lunch service, and a dinner service, I recommend emptying down the machine between breakfast and lunch and again between lunch and dinner. This means that the wash water will be fresh for each new service. This would not be applicable if you use a dishwasher that has a 'fill and dump' method of functioning, like some American machines. Certain dishwashers that are now on the market are designed to remove heavy soil before the actual wash cycle.

20. Do not close the door or hood overnight when the machine is switched off. At the end of service, the machine should be wiped down with a damp cloth and the door or hood should be left open. It allows the air to circulate and for the machine to dry out. This is important in the fight against bacteria building up inside of your machine. Dishwashers and glasswashers are hot and moist and this, combined with yeasts from beer, sugars from cocktails, etc building up, becomes a perfect breeding ground for bacteria to grow. This is especially important with glasswashers in night clubs or function suites that are used only a couple of nights each week and then left closed for the remainder of the time. This coupled with the fact that the lighting is usually low in nightclub bars, can result in exceptionally unhygienic circumstances and can lead to customers getting food poisoning or worse,

as mould spores can rapidly spread inside the machine and go unnoticed. Shine a torch inside your nightclub or function suite glasswasher and you may get a nasty surprise at what you find. Your customers aren't just getting a hangover the next day, you may be poisoning them.

21. Check the inside of the dishwasher hood for plastic tub lids. This is not that tragic although when the lids sit in the same place for a while, they become a hiding place for bacteria. On top of this, when the KP lifts the hood of the dishwasher to pull out the clean basket, water should run along these purpose-built grooves inside the hood and back into the wash tank of the machine. If these are blocked then water will pour out at a different angle and end up on the floor, posing a hazard within your kitchen.

22. Don't ignore the 'salt' light for the integral water softener. If the machine has a built-in water softener with an indicator light to alert staff to refill the softener with salt, when it flashes, they should top it up. Failing to do so will put years onto your machine and it won't be long until elements start to fail on a regular basis. If the machine doesn't have an indicator, build a routine so that staff check the salt levels on a regular basis. This applies to external water softeners too. If you have a machine with an inbuilt softener and you operate in an area with soft water, then you can turn this indicator

light off (in the user manual or ask your service engineer).

23. Using the door as a step ladder to reach shelves above the machine is a mistake. Believe me, this happens. I know a restaurant owner who caught a member of staff standing on the open dishwasher door and using it to get something from the shelf above. The door was already buckled, and other members of staff were complaining that it wasn't shutting properly. No wonder! I'm sure that it wouldn't be covered under the manufacturer's warranty.

24. Never hand wash dishes and glasses in the sink with dishwasher detergent. Because of the strength of these chemicals, staff should wear gloves and safety specs when changing over machine dishwasher detergent and rinse aid. They should never use these in a sink, even when wearing gloves.

25. Do not pour detergent into the wash tank. On rare occasions, we hear of staff manually putting in detergent every few washes when the detergent dosing unit is not working. We do not recommend doing so as splashes can cause serious burns. Even swapping over an empty bottle of dishwasher detergent with a full one should be treated with caution and the operator doing so should be wearing gloves and eye protection to minimise any physical damage caused by accidental splashes.

These are the main examples that I could think of, but I'm pretty sure you have witnessed a few traits that haven't been mentioned here. Do not underestimate the cost implications of your staff making these mistakes and chances are high that they are making far more mistakes than just one. The bottom line is that if you can identify bad practice, understand the harm that it does, and change it to good habits then that's a major win for your business.

7
Educating Your Staff

'Train people well enough so they can leave. Treat them well enough so they don't want to.'
— Sir Richard Branson

As stated before, this book is not meant to be an exhaustive recruitment guide. There are bookshelves bursting at the seams with information on finding great people and how to hire the best fit for your business. Don't underestimate just how important your staff are in not only your dishwashing process but to the whole of your operation. A dishwasher basket cannot load itself, put itself through the machine, bring the dishes back out and stack the clean plates away ready to be used again (not yet anyway). It needs an operator to do these tasks.

Have you ever asked yourself the following questions: How do your staff view you? How do you view your staff? What is your work culture like? Do they often go above and beyond, or do they appear to just come in to collect a wage?

Train your staff – they are your missing link. If they believe in you and what your restaurant stands for, then you will certainly develop a higher level of customer satisfaction through brilliant staff. Great employees are assets to your business, not liabilities. Hire slowly, and fire quickly. The good guys in your kitchen will respect the process and take pride in their job, but only if they are appreciated.

If you don't already have them onboard, hire and know how to retain great bar staff and KPs. If you don't know how to do this then I suggest that you learn or seek expert help. These guys will be happy to learn and improve your systems to get their dishwasher 'battle stations' working to maximum efficiency.

Effective workers take pride in what they do. They understand how vital their role is to the overall experience that you are trying to create for your customers. It is integral to the business so you must let the good ones know how much they are valued for them to succeed at their job.

Get tried and tested systems in place so that everyone knows their role. If they understand that they can have an impact on your systems, they will work smarter. You will find that staff take their work seriously when they understand the crucial function that they play in the bigger picture that you are creating.

How clean is your dishwashing machine? Do you know the answer to this question? If you don't have time for checking this on a regular basis, then make sure a few of your staff have it written into their job descriptions. Ensure that it is cleaned out daily, and that it is then checked by one of your staff at least once a week. This will create a great routine for making sure the machines are cleaned properly and as they become familiar with the machines, they may quickly notice something broken. Identifying a problem early before it breaks down on a Saturday afternoon and becomes a major issue is ideal.

I'm urging you to recognise the important role your kitchen and bar staff play. If your staff can genuinely be trusted to carry out the cleaning and care of the machine and dishwash area, including the points already mentioned, then they are worth their weight in gold, as the saying goes.

Lessons learned

I have dealt with all sorts of establishments in the catering and hospitality industry over the years and this includes schools and canteens in both the private and public sector. The staff in most of these schools are what you would term as 'old school' in their approach to kitchen hygiene and how they look after their dishwashers. I have taken out machines that are twenty-five years old that have to be retired because the parts are no longer available for them. Some of these machines looked like they were only a few months old because they were so well looked after.

The people in these institutions take pride in their equipment and go to great lengths to make sure that they are cleaning it properly. They listen to the advice of engineers and learn the tips and tricks of how to get the best out of their machines. They are the masters of 'sweating their assets'.

This is in direct contrast to machines that are in newer restaurants that have a high turnover of staff or where these staff are not looked after or properly trained. I have installed new dishwashers where, after the machine has been in for a few months, we get call-backs and the kitchen dishwash staff have changed. The machine looks like it has been in for a few years and it is clogged up with debris. It doesn't work properly, and the owner is frustrated because they have spent money on a machine that doesn't give them the desired results. They are looking for someone to blame and often the engineers can take the brunt of it as they represent the company from which it was purchased.

After we have cleaned the machine out, we explain the situation diplomatically. These calls are chargeable as they are due to user error and not covered under normal parts and labour warranty. However, we allow a bit of leeway and usually let them off the first time. But we do see this pattern repeat itself. If this sounds familiar to you, then try and take a leaf out of the book of the institution generation, and move closer to clearer profits.

Your new wash area plan

You have much to consider with regards to your dishwasher and the systems that either compliment or detract from it. In Part Three, you will be guided through the steps that I have developed which will take you from your existing setup (even if it doesn't exist yet) through to an ideal setup that will enhance your kitchen and the overall restaurant experience for your guests. I provide insight into what the results are when these steps are not followed and when I've witnessed corners being cut in the attempt to save time or money. Finally, we'll look at what the future holds for the commercial dishwasher and glasswasher industry and what direction this is headed in for the good or the bad of our industry and our planet.

PART THREE

THE FIVE-STEP WASH CYCLE METHODOLOGY

8
Beat The Competition

Owning and operating a restaurant is difficult and not for the faint-hearted. Competition in the food sector and in the catering and hospitality industry is tough. It's not just competition from other restaurants either. Theatres, cinemas, takeaways, and supermarkets are all vying for their slice of the market. Any option that gets someone to part with their hard-earned cash as opposed to spending it while delighting in the surroundings of your fine establishment is competition.

Be it a night in with a pizza and beer in front of the latest box set or setting aside money for a summer holiday, you have to work hard to keep your customers happy enough so that they rave about you, recommend you to others, and keep returning for more of your hospitality. Take advantage of the marginal gains that are hidden within your restaurant, and when you are planning on renewing your dishwashing system, the following steps will go a long way.

The five-step wash cycle methodology

1. Current setup – examine in detail what you currently have

2. Clarity – where your business is going, your dishwasher options and what else is available

3. Cost – what budget have you allocated, which finance options are out there

4. Create – what to expect when you choose and install a new system

5. Clean dishes, clear profits –the juicy bit where it all comes together through training, maintenance, and review

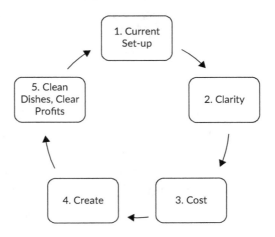

How to use this model

To get the best use out of this model, I recommend that you read it all the way through first to get an understanding of how the steps work and how they overlap slightly at the edges. There will be things that are glaringly obvious and other gems that will make you take note. Either way, I hope you get beneficial use from this methodology.

9
Step 1: Current Setup

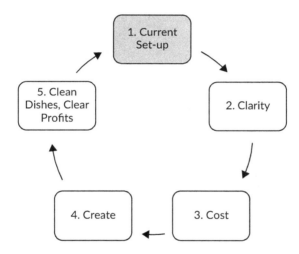

This first step is a fact-finding exercise which allows you to examine your motivation for changing your current setup. There are many dishwasher and glass-washer manufacturers out there and each of them have multiple models for sale. Some of this information applies to both types of machinery but for ease of use I've concentrated on your dishwasher.

Having a good think about your current dishwasher setup is key to getting the most out of this process. This first step is still relevant even if you don't have a current setup and are starting from scratch with a new venture. It may be that you have recently taken over premises that already have a dishwash system in place. Whatever you have setup at present, this will be worth a read.

For the sake of simplicity let's assume you already have a system in place and you know that it is inefficient and underperforming. If you are starting from the beginning, it is crucial to reiterate that you will regret leaving the dishwasher as an afterthought. Read through these steps to understand how important your dishwasher and supporting systems are on your new restaurant setup.

Evaluation

Consider your plans for the future of your restaurant. Go through the following points. Ask yourself the questions that the points pose and be honest with your answers.

How busy are you?

Are you located in a city centre, a high street, a busy shopping centre or mall, where you have a constant stream of potential customers walking by your door?

Are you located in a more rural location and you rely on seasonal tourism at your peak times? Do the busy times take care of the non-existent customers during the winter period?

Whether you fall into city centre or rural location, you must plan your dishwasher to handle your busiest times. That way it can cope well with your maximum demand and sail through the easier times too. How does your current machine perform when you are at your busiest?

Plans to modify

What volume of covers (bums on seats) can you accommodate at present and what volume increase (if any) you would like to achieve in the next five years? Are you going to be extending the venue or kitchen to make more room for tables and chairs? Are you looking to expand your kitchen because it's too small to cope with your demand, or are you going to steal some kitchen space to allow more customers in? Is the place going to become smaller? What available space will be allocated to the dishwash area? Will you upsize, downsize, or stay the same? Do your KPs have enough room to manoeuvre around to effectively perform at their best, or are they constantly bumping into each other?

When your existing machine was performing at its best, could it cope with the volume of dishes when you

CLEAN DISHES, CLEAR PROFITS

were at your busiest, such as on Mother's Day, bank holiday weekends, etc? Are you drastically changing your menu? Are you needing more or less kitchen space because of this? Will there be other equipment needed because of this change or will you be getting rid of equipment as you downsize?

The positives and negatives of your existing system

Examine your current system. What are the positives and negatives? For example, there may not be enough area for set-down of dirty dishes. Observe the process during a busy lunch and dinner service, and I suggest you repeat this a few times when there are different staff working at different shift times. Ask the staff and get their honest feedback. After all, they are the ones on the front line.

The best way to find out the ins and outs of your existing system is to put in a few shifts yourself. If you've never done it before, it is a real eye opener and will give you some great insights into the stresses involved when you have hundreds of dishes to turn around from dirty to clean in a short space of time. There's a high chance that you'll enjoy it too.

The KPs may be particular in how they do things in the kitchen, but it will give you the opportunity to tactfully ask why certain tasks are performed in certain ways. It's a fascinating exercise to observe how staff use your current system as it reveals the good points and bad points in both the setup and how they use it. Do they have refined a system that works well already, or have they had to make do with a failing machine and are working around these restrictions?

Most kitchens only stock around two-thirds of the dishes they need, so a fast turnaround is critical to ensure a smooth service. Getting an insight into the workings of the dishwash area and how this integral cog in the wheel of your restaurant fits into the bigger picture will help you to appreciate just how vital it is.

External help

Do you have a dishwasher company you currently work with that you like and trust? Someone who understands the importance of this piece of kit and its supporting surrounds? Can you lift the phone and receive consultation and details around your existing setup? Do you know someone with experience and fresh ideas that can help with the positives and negatives around what you have?

Take note of what works well and needs to remain or be replicated in your new setup. There may be some of your setup that does what is needed and although you are making changes, it must remain or be replaced well. Whether it is a new site or existing system being replaced, what way does it flow? Do the dirties arrive at one end and are cleans handled at the other end? Is the current run from left to right, or from right to left? Should this remain the same or be switched around? Consult your staff and your dishwasher engineer. They will be able to offer insights that you haven't even considered.

What doesn't work well and why? Document your findings so that you don't forget. Are there practices that appear time-consuming? Could these be improved upon and refined? Would a new setup help with this?

I've seen large conveyor dishwashers being taken out of kitchens only to be replaced by smaller more modern and efficient passthrough dishwashers because the owner decided to use some of the kitchen space as a customer viewing area. Guests could sit and observe the workings of the kitchen whilst being wined and dined. It's a great selling point and this type of theatre kitchen experience is on the increase. Could this work for your place?

It's a difficult decision to work out what space to allocate to your guests, and what space you will need to allow for staff to prepare and cook their food and everything that goes with this process, including all equipment and working space. Real estate costs are generally always on the rise and the best way to meet your constant outgoings is to get as many customers through your doors as possible.

It is a balancing act though so if you are in any doubt when it comes to dishing out the square metres, seek expert advice from an architect or designer so that the kitchen doesn't suffer for the sake of a few extra seats. Whatever the changes, your kitchen must be able to deliver the requirements of your menu.

It may just be the fact that your current dishwasher has given up. It has broken down or been repaired for the last time, and you know that it is time to upgrade to a newer model. Go through the questions above before you commit to buying in haste. If you under-stand your objectives at this stage, you can move to the next step with what you want to achieve.

10
Step 2: Clarity

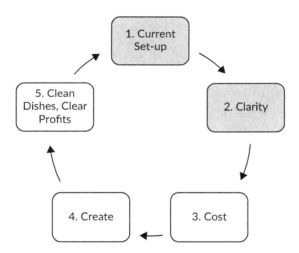

This next step helps you find clarity on the options that are available to you, so you can build a picture of what you want to achieve. Maybe it has been years since you last researched buying a new dishwasher or this may be your first time. I suppose it's a bit like the dating game; a lot has changed but the fundamentals are still the same.

Again, we must start with asking more questions. Who is going to help you with this project? Which suppliers will you approach? Do you have an incumbent dishwash company that already looks after your machines?

Whichever one you decide on, it's a good idea to keep most of the work with one company or one point of contact. This helps when it comes to ordering, installation, snagging, and training, which we'll cover later.

Try to get a site survey of your dishwash area conducted by a professional. This will include the access and exit of machinery and equipment, your current services (electrical, water and waste), and will help you figure out if your existing stainless-steel tabling will fit your new dishwasher, or will you need new, better tabling? What type of machine do you need? What features do you want it to have to bring what type of benefit to your business, eg energy saving over its lifetime? Is our environment and sustainability a factor you want to consider? It may become legislation and therefore, it's best to at least keep it in mind. This can shape your decision about which machine is better for you in the long term.

Request drawings of potential dishwasher setups and do your homework. Can you visit other sites that have a great setup that you know about or that have been recommended by a manufacturer or your supplier? Can you get examples of their work?

This stage also includes making sure that the appropriate services are in place eg the electrical supply to the dishwasher – does it need upgraded or downgraded? What size of area have you got to work with? Is this set in stone or can you expand it?

Understanding your dishwash options

Trying to decide which make and model of dishwasher is the best for your restaurant is complicated. There are many to choose from, and this includes which physical type to go for if you are setting up a restaurant from scratch. By physical type I mean choosing between a front loader, a passthrough, a rack conveyor, etc. At this stage you should ask yourself how you want to proceed. Here are three options:

Do it myself

This is DIY where you do the research and leg work around what is available and what will be the best fit for you. This option is time-consuming and your time could be better spent elsewhere. This choice can often be a false economy.

Do it with me

This is a bit like the first option although you are drafting in some expert help. If your time is precious and you still like to keep your hand in with the big decisions, then this option is for you.

Do it for me

In this instance you use a reputable company that you trust to work with your staff to make decisions that will deliver the best outcome for your business. If handled correctly, this option will save you time and money in the long run.

There are positives and negatives for whichever route you choose to go down and only you will know which one is best for you and your situation. What period of time will be allowed for with regards to snagging once a new machine is installed? If you buy purely on price and don't factor this in, you will pay for someone to come back out and re-educate staff or fix something that has gone wrong because it isn't being operated properly. Discuss this with your supplier so that you know where you stand with this.

A great setup

To make things easier, the following guide points out the ideal dishwasher setup. This is based on a passthrough dishwasher and I have laid this out as a left to right configuration, but it would be easy to flip around if your dishwash area works with a right to left flow. This process works with a corner installation too. The process is simple when it is broken down, but it must work in practice. Fortunately, it does work, and I've seen variations of it in different restaurants thousands of times over the years. Simple is usually best, and when it works well, it is highly effective in delivering the right results.

Dirties set-down

When your waiting staff enter your kitchen wash-up area with a stack of dirty cups, plates, etc, they need somewhere to set these down. This may be part of your dishwasher inlet tabling or a separate table that leads in before the inlet tabling. Ideally it will be a gantry style that allows for more surface area so that they don't run out of space at peak times.

It's great practice for the dirties to be stacked in piles as they are set down. This may take a waiter a few more seconds but it helps the KP immensely. It also helps five minutes later when other waiting staff are not having to balance their dirty plates on top of gravy jugs, tiny saucers, etc. I've often seen it look like a game of Jenga and one false move can wipe out around £100 worth of crockery. Your system will benefit if you get this right.

Bins and waste disposal units

There are normally two bins around or underneath the dirties set-down area. One is for used napkins, butter and sauce packs, etc, and the other is for food waste. Have your waiting staff or KP scrape the plates as thoroughly as possible. The less food waste that goes down the sinks or into the dishwasher, the better.

Have a bucket handy around this area so that the left-over liquid in cups, mugs, milk jugs, and slops can be emptied. A 10-litre bucket with a handle is a good size, doesn't need to be emptied too often, and can be transported easily to be emptied.

It is worth speaking briefly about waste disposal units and waste food digesters at this point. These are contraptions that waste food can be placed into. They grind up food and the resulting slurry is disposed of down the drain system along with running water. They are still in use in certain areas although some local authorities have banned them. At time of writing, they are completely banned in Scotland where food waste must be collected and transported to a municipal digester.[8] In Northern Ireland there are regulations around the control of trade effluents which must be adhered to.[9] At present there are no plans to ban waste disposal units in England or Wales.

I strongly advise that you take advice on this with your local Environmental Health Officer (EHO) or local authority before purchasing a unit, as they are good at

---

8   The Waste (Scotland) Regulations 2012: www.legislation.gov.uk/ sdsi/2012/9780111016657

9   Water and Sewerage Services (Northern Ireland) Order 2006: www. legislation.gov.uk/nisi/2006/3336/contents

what they do but it would be a waste of money if you are not permitted to use one.

Cutlery soak

Such a simple thing that is often overlooked is the cutlery soak. It is nothing fancy, just a small bucket or 5-litre open tub with hot water and mild detergent. This allows the dirty cutlery to soak so the remaining food particles do not harden and the cutlery then cleans easier in the dishwasher.

Inlet tabling

Next in line is the dishwasher inlet tabling. To recap, this is the stainless-steel tabling that runs into the dishwasher. It will normally have at least one sink and preferably two if you have the space. The inlet tabling usually comes with an under shelf, where cleaning chemicals and dishwasher chemicals can sit for easy access. The edge of the tabling furthest away from the dishwasher should be slightly higher than the lip that ties into the dishwasher to allow water to run towards the machine and not collect in the corners.

Water softener

If the machine does not come with an integral water softener and one is needed because you are in an area of hard water, then an external softener will be placed

CLEAN DISHES, CLEAR PROFITS

in line with the water supply feed to the dishwasher. This could be at either side of the machine depending on available space. The same principle will apply to a reverse osmosis unit and any other water treatment unit.

Sinks

Double sinks are always preferred in case of machine downtime in future. The sinks are enclosed within the inlet tabling and have a back to front depth of around 400mm. This doubles as a basket-loading area and can't be so large that the baskets fall into the sinks. The plugs for these sinks are a type of standpipe that inserts into the plug hole and when it is pulled out, there is a stainless-steel mesh guard that prevents any solids from going down the plug hole and creating a blockage. In the case of a glasswasher sink, have something similar like a mesh or a 5-litre (one gallon) container with holes in the bottom of it to catch straws, lemon slices, etc from blocking up the sink plug hole.

Pre-spray

The pre-spray is a great addition to your dishwasher setup. It is essentially a shower that hangs overhead and you can spray down the dirty dishes before they go into the dishwasher. It is a first wet for the plates which also loosens and dislodges food particles and gets rid of any soap from the cutlery that has been soaking in the soapy basin, prior to it going into the dishwasher.

There are different variations of this, and the one that I recommend has both a hot and cold feed with a 12-inch faucet attached. If you have double sinks, the pre-spray sits towards the back in the middle and the faucet can swivel across both sinks and can be tucked back to allow for the passage of taller items in the dishwasher baskets as they pass towards the machine.

Dishwasher

For this type of setup that we are running through, the dishwasher would be at least a single hood passthrough machine. Inlet and outlet tabling can also be used with double hood passthrough and conveyor dishwashers. It wouldn't work as efficiently with a frontloading dishwasher.

For this to work well, the dishwasher profile has to match the profile edge of the stainless-steel inlet and outlet tabling. If it's all part of a new project or setup, then have this discussion with your stainless-steel fabricator. They can manufacture the lipped edge of the tabling to suit.

The hood of the dishwasher is lifted by the KP and the basket full of dishes is slid from the inlet tabling into the dishwasher from the side. The basket rests on the basket support inside the machine and the operator closes the hood and it immediately kicks into a cycle.

For a corner installation of a passthrough dishwasher, it works the same. It just means that the basket will be loaded into the side or the front of the machine and the basket support guide rail will be adjusted on install to accommodate a corner situation. A note on corner dishwashers for your installation engineer – try and have the front panel of the dishwasher accessible for future service engineer visits, and with some machines you may need regular access to a USB port for data collection.

Once the machine has washed and rinsed the dishes and the cycle is complete, the basket moves into the clean side of the operation. The hood is lifted, and the basket slides out of the opposite side from where it went in, and in the case of a corner installation, it will be pulled out at a 90° angle to the side it went in.

Outlet tabling

Like the inlet tabling, the outlet tabling lips into the exit side of the dishwasher and has a boxed edge which fits the industry standard size of the baskets to make a smooth transition from dishwasher to exit tabling (as it is also known). It is angled up higher at the far side from the machine so that run-off water can stream effectively back in the direction of the dishwasher.

In larger setups, there are gantry shelves above the outlet tabling which can house the cutlery baskets to ensure that they are dry before being put away. Do not ask staff to lift baskets full of dishes and cups much higher that waist height because of how much these things weigh. The upright cutlery baskets, however, are ideal for this. Sometimes the dishwasher detergent and rinse aid are located next to the exit table. The dishwasher automatically draws these in through their appropriate tubes.

Bank of runners

A bank of runners is a storage solution for dishwasher baskets when they are not being used. This can be manufactured into the inlet or outlet tabling, although it's more commonly located under the surface of the outlet tabling. The main reason for this location choice is because most wash areas in kitchens are tight for space and a double sink tends to take up most of the space in an inlet table.

Grease trap

Whichever way the flow of the wastewater from the sinks and dishwasher is directed, a grease trap can be fitted in this location. This is a good time to specify one in as they are difficult to retrospectively fit once the new setup has been fully installed. Do not place it directly after the dishwasher, make sure that it catches the sink water too.

In cases where there is no space to fit even a small grease trap, a small pump which feeds a drain enzyme into the pipes during the night when the system is shut down is better than having no grease management system at all. The bacteria create a culture that breaks down the grease build-up. There are now grease traps on the market that are extremely effective in removing the FOG (fats, oils, and grease) in a hygienic manner and are better for our environment.

Trolley or shelving for clean plates

When the clean dishes, cups, and cutlery exit the machine and dry on the outlet tabling, they are lifted directly onto shelves or transferred onto trolleys to be transported to shelves, ready to be used again in service. This must be easily accessible for the kitchen staff, so that they can plate up without any delays to the operation.

Other considerations

When you are considering which machine to buy, take note of the following information to help make your choice. Listen to experts on the subject, but also listen to what your inner voice is telling you. If you are environmentally conscious then you will want to look at the energy efficiency and the long-term energy use and life expectancy of a new machine. There may be a trade-off as energy efficient models can be more expensive in their upfront costs but cheaper to run when in operation. Ask the manufacturers and do your homework here, unless you're happy with the 'Do it for me' model detailed earlier.

Does the machine have to be quiet? Features such as thermal and acoustic insulation are important when it comes to your glasswasher. The glasswasher is usually in the front of house part of your restaurant in your bar area, so it is a good idea to consider if you need the machine to be quiet. This will depend on your restaurant's ambience. Are you an upbeat and trendy restaurant that aims to attract a young crowd with loud music being played through your PA system or are you fine dining, with low volume music (or none at all)?

If the latter is the case, consider a glasswasher with acoustic insulation. These will typically be double-skinned machines with a double-skinned door. When the machine is performing a cycle, it will do so more quietly than its single-skinned counterpart. It will cost more but is worth the investment as it will also save on energy costs as the double skin serves to retain heat energy.

Another energy efficiency method that some dishwashers employ is the use of drain heat recovery, where heat energy is reduced as the machine uses the hot drain wastewater system to raise the temperature of the incoming water feed. Consider how much water consumption the machine requires every cycle and if it is more economical with its chemical usage. The overall lifecycle costs of your new machine will be important once it is in full operational mode, and of course reliability and price are major factors to keep in mind.

11
Site Survey

A site survey should be carried out at this stage in the proceedings. Your dishwasher company should carry out one for you although if you follow the points below you will gain some insight by doing it yourself. If you have not done one before, then this will be an excellent guide in how to carry out a site survey for a glasswasher, an under counter dishwasher, or a hood type dishwasher. Carry this book with you for reference. I have tried to think of everything that I've come across before on-site surveys to help you.

You don't want to order a new glasswasher or dishwasher and when the equipment arrives it does not fit through the doors of your premises, or you order a three-phase electric dishwasher and you only have single-phase power available. These are only a few examples of mistakes you can avoid.

There are five main issues to consider when you are carrying out a site survey which cover the bases in going from your current setup to your future setup:

- Access and exit (new machine in, old machine out)

- Electrical supply

- Water supply (hot or cold pressure, hardness/softness of water supply)

- Wastewater outlet (height and diameter)

- Who will be present to help lift or move the machine

To get an answer to the issues that you will face, you should arm yourself with the following tools:

- Pen or pencil and paper

- Measuring tape (that measures in cm and mm) and the width × depth × height of the machine and space available

- Torch (for looking under sinks, behind machines, and into dimly lit fuse boxes). The torch on your mobile phone will work well enough for this purpose

- This book to help you

Access for your new dishwasher and/or glasswasher

This is extremely important. Once you have decided where the glasswasher and/or dishwasher will be located and operate from, check to make sure that it will fit through all doors to the wash area and safely get to where you want it to be. Are there any stairs that need to be negotiated?

Remember that if you have an existing machine that is being replaced, consider the 'access' measurements for the exit of your old ware washer. If it is a hood type or passthrough dishwasher, take width sizes from handle to handle. Doors may need to be removed to accommodate a passthrough dishwasher.

There may have been renovations to the commercial kitchen or bar since the old machine was installed years earlier – don't assume that because one fitted in before that it can be removed easily. Always measure! It will save time and stress on install day. Check that you have the details of the machine dimensions. Take note of these sizes and make sure that it will fit before placing your order. If you don't have them, ask your supplier.

Who will be there to help move or lift the machine? Plan the route that the machine will take to get to its destination. Who will be available to help if the old glasswasher (as well as the new one) must be lifted over a bar before being installed? In my time, I have seen all sorts of crazy scenarios. One time a new passthrough dishwasher was ordered and it was assumed because the new one would fit through the door to the commercial kitchen, then the old one would be removed without any hassle. However, the old dishwasher had a side box on it that was semi hidden because of the inlet tabling, and the salesman had failed to notice and account for it. It was also rusted on so couldn't be removed on-site. The result was that the industrial passthrough dishwasher had to be lifted horizontally and fitted through the serving hatch, which was wider than the door, but four feet off the ground. That was not a one-man job, let me assure you!

Electrical supply for the ware washer

You will need to know the following:

- How is the existing machine wired? Is it on a 13-amp plug or is it hard wired into a rotary switch or terminal?

- Where is the fuse to isolate the machine and what is its rating? For example, is it 25-amp, 32-amp, or higher?

- If it works off a single fuse, then the machine is single-phase. Is it a three-phase machine with 3 × 16-amp fuses, 3 × 20-amp fuses or higher?

If the machine is being upgraded to a more powerful one, then an electrician will upgrade the fuse, the supply cable (from 2.5mm to 6mm twin and earth) and switches. The supply cable is the cable from the fuse box to the socket or terminal next to where the machine will be positioned.

This is an area where your local electrician should be able to help you if you need further assistance. Luckily, most of the machines nowadays are multipower and can be switched on-site to accommodate your current setup. They can then be later changed if you decide to upgrade the electrical supply.

If it is a clear site that the machine is going into, always go for a higher-rated fuse to get the most out of the machine. This applies to multipower machines and will not apply to some glasswashers that only come with a 13-amp supply.

Water supply for the dishwasher or glasswasher

In your restaurant, you should already know where the mains water supply into the building is located. If you don't know where it is, find out. The ideal scenario is that your new machine will have a high pressure (2-5 Bar), hot water feed (60°C max) going into it. This requires less time and energy to heat, especially between cycles when you are at your busiest. This is not always the case as hot water usually comes from a boiler and the pressure is lower than cold water from the mains supply.

The water feed into the machine determines how the rinse arms rotate during the final rinse of each cycle, although this may be irrelevant on machines with an air gap (a break in the water to prevent backflow of water from machine into the water mains). These machines will have an inbuilt boost pump to allow for this.

You can test the water pressure with a pressure tester. Alternatively, if you turn on a water tap that is on the same plumbing as the dishwasher water feed, then you can tell if there is good pressure present or not. Always try your hot and cold taps.

This is where there is normally a trade-off. For example, take these two dishwashers:

1. Low hot water pressure – dishwasher would need a rinse booster pump but may only need to be plugged into an electrical socket with a three-pin thirteen amp plug.

2. Good cold water pressure – dishwasher would not need a rinse booster pump, but would work better on a 25- or 32-amp hard wire plug (with 6mm twin and earth cable).

Choosing between these two machines may then come down to price.

Water hardness may be an issue depending on where in the UK your premises are located. You most likely have an idea of whether you need a water softener with your machine. If you are in doubt, ask your local water authority, buy water hardness testing strips online, or simply check your kettle. If the water in your area is hard, there will be a white or brown scale build-up in and around the element in the kettle or urn. If this is the case, then you will need a water softener with your machine. Most ware washers, except for small glasswashers, can be supplied with integral water softeners. Otherwise you will have to purchase a stand-alone water softener.

Dishwasher with a drain pump? (wastewater outlet)

Does your existing machine drain away when the stand pipe (plug) is pulled out or do you press a button to activate the drain pump? If it's with a drain pump, make sure the new machine you order has a drain pump. If not fitted as standard, it will be available as an option.

For frontloading dishwashers, the other option is to mount it on a stand if you have the height available. If there is a high plumbing waste standpipe –

the machine going in this space would need a drain pump. If you do not have an existing commercial glasswasher or dishwasher, then consider that the outlet for the waste will come out at the bottom of the machine at its lowest point. When the machine is in position, will this be above or below the height of the waste pipe that the drain hose goes into? Remember: water cannot flow up unless helped by a drain pump.

Are you replacing a frontloading dishwasher with a hood type dishwasher?

If so, measure out the available width and height above where the old machine sits. Shelving may have to be removed or relocated to accommodate the added height of the hood of the new dishwasher when it is open. There may be more steam emitted from your new passthrough dishwasher and so a canopy may have to be fitted above where the machine will sit. Certain manufacturers have passthrough dishwashers that come with a four-sided hood which keeps the steam contained within the hood and does away with the need for a canopy.

Ask yourself again – why are you upgrading? Is your old machine broken, are you building an extension, or do you anticipate greater volume that the old one couldn't cope with? Asking yourself these questions will help you make a better decision about which machine is right for you. If this all seems too much, speak to your supplier and they will help you through the process. Remember: Keeping your old one as back up is an option if it was working and you have enough room to store it.

One machine or two?

Wetherspoons pubs each have two glasswashers at the side of their bar. Having two machines helps to cope with volume at peak times and as a backup if one of them breaks down suddenly. Having two dishwashers is real peace of mind. But these must be set out correctly so that the workflow makes sense and dirties and cleans don't cross over and mix. Having two machines would be an extreme luxury for the majority of restaurants as most places are tight for both physical space and cash.

12
Step 3: Cost

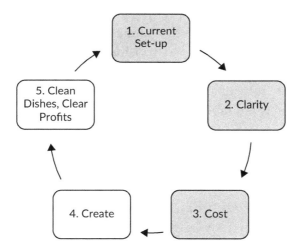

When we talk about cost, we're talking about how much you would *like* to spend and how much you will *actually* spend on a new dishwashing system. At this crucial stage, begin with the end in mind – invest well and get it correct for the future of your business. This is an important piece in the jigsaw. When I ask someone what their budget is for a dishwasher project or ask how much they are able or willing to spend, the common answer is 'as little as possible'. Of course, no one wants to overspend more than they need to and this step in the process is critical as it can make or break everything and undo the steps before and the steps that follow.

I don't tend to tackle this subject first. Every establishment is different and I'm not in the habit of supplying a one-size-fits-all stainless-steel box that cleans dishes. I go through the previous steps with the client and we draw out a wish list because if we have to make a price compromise somewhere, then we have multiple components to consider where changes in specification can be made. A hard-working and busy commercial kitchen deserves the best dishwasher that you can reasonably afford.

Projects

With any project that is being undertaken, price or cost plays an integral part in how it plays out. Other elements include the project scope, quality, and time.

Harry Sneed, a pioneer in software testing technology and professor for software engineering, developed a model that illustrates these variables at play and called it 'The Devil's Quadrangle of Project Management'.[10]

---

10 Ariane von Berg (2015) 'The Magic Triangle and Devil's Quadrangle', www.inloox.com/company/blog/articles/the-magic-triangle-and-devil-s-quadrangle-understanding-project-management-models

Sneed links all four factors and argues that the distinction of the quality factor means that if a cut in quality of the project results can be accepted, the quantitative scope of the project could be increased while staying within the ideal time frame and budget. On the other hand, in order to maintain expected quality and scope of a project, an increase of costs will incur if there is a time quench.

Changes in one parameter always affect one or more of the remaining factors, leading to a changing form of the quadrangle. The overall size of the quadrangle, however, doesn't change no matter what shape it takes. To put it simply, if you squeeze too tight on the price, something else will have to give. You really do want the full project to be delivered with all four constraints being met.

Consider the whole picture. You are investing in the company that will help you with this project. Give them the time and the money that they need to carry out the project to your desired outcome. Remember that most businesses are like you. They only want the best for their staff and their customers and would like to make a decent living along the way. Please don't buy on price alone on something this important to your business as it will have a detrimental effect on the outcome.

That being said, there's no harm in asking for a discount. You may have a rough idea of how much you can spend at the top end of your budget and luckily, there are loads of financial options these days that can help you proceed with the best kit available.

How to purchase a new dishwashing system

There are now multiple options available to businesses for owning or using capital equipment in their premises. If you are serious about this project, you can become creative and resourceful and find a way for it to happen. Remember, depending on the legal status of your business (private limited, limited partnership), you can claim tax relief on the purchase as it is a piece of capital equipment that will sit on the balance sheet as an asset. You can claim back the VAT that you have paid but I highly recommend that you speak first with your accountant to find out the best option for your business.

There are various ways to affordably own a new dishwasher and tabling or a new glasswasher. Your dishwasher is the beating heart behind the smooth operation of a commercial kitchen, as a glasswasher is to a successful working bar. However, they are often overlooked until something goes wrong and they break down. Inevitably this will be during busy service on a Saturday night and is a nightmare. Often, you will not have budgeted for a new machine, and will be faced with having to buy a new dishwasher or glasswasher when you least expected it. There are times when buying a machine outright is not best for your business.

Finance, leasing, or credit are great options for a commercial kitchen to have, as sometimes it is not as viable to spend the cash associated with such a capital equipment purchase. There are pros and cons for each so I'll lay out some points below and you can go through them and see what best suits your individual circumstance at both a personal and a business level. The following list is not exhaustive, but it gives you a good indication as to what options are available. Always remember the VAT.

Cash

Paying by cash means that you have the cash available to buy outright. This covers paying by cheque, BACS transfer payments, and the like.

On account

This is where your supplier allows you some time before they expect payment to be made. A typical timeframe for this is thirty days before you must pay.

Credit card

If you or your business has a good credit rating, then consider putting the purchase on a credit card. When it comes time to pay interest on the card, you can balance transfer onto a 0% interest card and pay it off over many months.

Finance and leasing

You can get a loan from your bank which will give you a way of paying it off over a set number of months or years, but you will most likely pay interest.

Some manufacturers offer their own finance and better still, some even have offers for 0% interest payment plans. These are structured over a few years and mean that apart from an administration fee, you pay off the same amount as you borrow. You own the equipment when the final bill is paid, and it helps with cashflow as there is not a large capital outlay involved.

Lease terms available vary between different leasing companies but are often over either three or five years and in certain circumstances a full parts and labour warranty can be included for the duration of the lease.

Some pros and cons of financing and leasing:

- No large capital outlay. You are using money from the operating budget, not the capital budget.

- You can buy the latest dishwashing or glasswashing machine to fit your needs.

- Available to start-ups and established businesses (different terms will apply).

- Available to sole traders, partnerships, and limited companies.

- You may pay a higher rate of interest and pay back more than you borrowed.

Other plus points to leasing new ware washing equipment include:

- Pay for installation separately or include it in the lease.

- Fixed, affordable monthly payments – with no hidden charges.

- The new equipment can be offset against tax – a major advantage. Often, this leads to you being able to buy a higher specified machine than you could afford.

At the end of the dishwasher lease period you will normally have the following options:

- Retain ownership of the equipment for an additional payment of a percentage of the net invoice value.

- Continue to use the equipment on a lease for a lower monthly fee.

- Return the equipment without penalty.

- Upgrade to new equipment by signing a new lease agreement.

All finance and lease agreements are subject to credit checks and will depend on your personal circumstances and that of your business. The length of time that you have been trading for is an important factor and usually means that companies trading less than three years (with only one or two year set of accounts) will typically pay more per month than a company with a strong and established trading history.

You may have to guarantee your primary place of residence (your home) against the finance or lease. This means that your house is at risk. If ever there was an incentive to make sure that you get the most out of your assets, then that is a strong one.

Rental

Renting is an option although you never own the equipment unless you come to an agreement with the rental company. Usually rental agreements cover wear and tear and parts and labour warranty, but do not cover user neglect, ie blocked filters, blocked pumps, etc.

Crowd funding

Crowd funding through your customers is also an option. TV chef Gary Usher has famously used crowd funding to raise money for various projects which include the fit out and opening of his restaurants and bistros. (Crowd funding is where money is raised through a group of independent lenders who are all willing to invest their cash in a project in order to get a return with interest.)

Reconditioned or 'upcycled' machines

If you lack the funds you need when it comes to paying for a new dishwasher, you can always consider a reconditioned machine. There are pros and cons of buying reconditioned, and one of the main points to remember is that someone else got rid of the machine for a reason. It depends on who has reconditioned the machine for you to buy. Can you get to see it working, even in a video? At least you're not contributing to our waste system by buying a preloved machine.

The list above is not financial advice. It is a simple guide that might present you with options that you hadn't previously considered. Buy the best you can afford and do it in advance of being forced to purchase at a crisis point.

I've touched on the fact that you might be coming into this process at the cash point out of desperation after your existing machine has already packed in and given up. If this is the case, I urge you to take a deep breath and at least read through our whole five-step process (if not the book) before rushing out and getting 'at least something in' before your next busy weekend.

We try and keep in touch during the time period where the finance is being sorted. This can be a challenging time for a business owner as they may have to produce a set of accounts and sometimes speaking with an accountant is a sobering experience. An accountant may not see the true value in investing thousands of pounds into a sleek dishwashing system. Ideally, you will buy the full setup under your one supplier. That way the next steps will run smoother. However, circumstances may dictate that you have to buy the full system in parts and pay for tabling and the likes separate from the machine purchase.

13
Step 4: Create

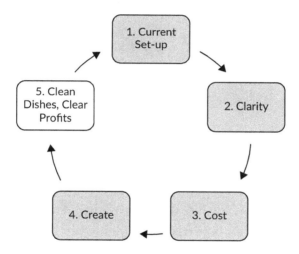

The correct installation of a commercial dishwasher is important, although in my experience it is often seen by restaurant owners as an expense that can be done without. The installation day and time will be crucial to minimising the disruption to your restaurant. You must break a few eggs to make an omelette and this will be the case here, so plan for the disruption. If in step three you've pushed the price down too far, it may impact how the installation is carried out. Give the supply and installation process the proper consideration that it deserves and you will make life easier for you and your staff.

I normally set the timescales and expectations of our clients at this stage. We will recap on a few key things: The machine and design layout agreed upon, the finance, when the order will be placed, delivery to us or them, tabling to us or them, and the best day and time for installation.

Consider the following factors:

When

Choose an agreed day and time that suits both you and the supply company. Overtime may have to be paid for the installation engineer if you want the work carried out of their normal working hours. It will have to be after any electrical adjustments have been made and once any other tradesmen have carried out their work (plumbing, flooring, etc).

By whom

Installing a commercial dishwasher is different from installing a domestic dishwasher. Therefore, I advise that it is carried out by the company that you are buying the machine from or carried out by the manufacturer or another reputable company.

In the installation literature, the regulations state that it must be carried out by a 'competent person' with a certain level of experience. Admittedly, this is rather vague. There are electrical skills, plumbing skills, and sometimes joinery skills needed to carry out this task. With no disrespect intended to the different trades, a specialist dishwashing company is highly recommended. Often an electrician or a plumber will not have the cross skills needed to install, commission, and test the machine to the correct standard.

I remember being called to a job where a plumber had installed a machine and were unable to drain it down. On closer inspection, the machine was bought without a drain pump and it turned out that the plumber did not have the skills or confidence to open the machine up and fix the problem. This is fair enough, although the fault lies with whoever originally specified and ordered the machine as it hadn't been properly surveyed.

Delivery company or installer?

If you are buying purely on price and possibly through an internet dealer, they may not offer installation. Instead, you may find that they only offer a delivery that is classed as a kerbside delivery. This means that the delivery driver is under no obligation to site the new machine in its box anywhere other than outside the door of the delivery address.

What implications would this have for you as a business? It may arrive during a busy lunchtime to sit out the front of your shop. We live in Britain, so there's a high chance that it will be raining. If the delivery driver is kind enough to drop the machine inside your premises, do you have enough storage room for the new machine to sit until it is able to be installed?

When you use a reputable company to source, deliver, and install your dishwasher, you will have more control over when it will arrive at your premises. As most manufacturers offer a standard twelve months parts and labour warranty, the installation must be carried out properly and to their standards. The manufacturers have decades of experience in this area whereby installations have been poorly executed and the new machine does not work as it should. This often results in the customer activating their warranty and placing a service call out for the manufacturer (or one of their trained subcontractors) to attend the site and rectify the 'fault'.

A large proportion of these call outs are because of an error in the way in which the machine has been installed, and when this is the case, the manufacturer then bills the customer for their time to rectify someone else's incorrect installation. Trying to save money at the front end will often cost you more at the back end. Make sure that your installation is carried out by someone that has experience in commercial dishwashers.

How long should installation take?

This depends on what you currently have and what your new setup is going to look like. For an under-counter dishwasher installation where we are swapping out an old machine for a new machine, we allow three to four hours to complete the job. There are logistics involved, including removing every piece of shrink-wrapped film from the body of the machine. This alone can take forty minutes to do properly. It must all be removed as over time it gets baked on and warps which allows bacteria to breed on the surface of the machine.

However, if there is tabling, sinks, and a larger passthrough or conveyor machine involved, then this process will take longer. For a conveyor machine it can take around two full working days to complete. Factor this in and discuss it at length with your installer, as this will lead you onto the next point.

Don't expect a 5-star installation service if you've paid for 3-star quality. If both you and your supplier have been reasonable with the installation negotiations, then they should work around your kitchen or bar and try to accommodate your staff as much as possible.

There will be a degree of disruption involved, but it's about having the conversation and preparing for it as much as possible. This may mean starting service at a slightly different time or finishing earlier than normal.

Your old dishwasher

What do you want to do with it? Would you like to try and recycle it, sell it to someone else online, or have it removed for scrap? Make sure your guys are aware of WEEE regulations which govern the scrapping of waste electrical and electronic equipment.[11]

---

11   Health and Safety Executive Guidance (2018) 'Waste Electrical and Electronic Equipment Recycling', www.hse.gov.uk/waste/waste-electrical.htm

14
Step 5: Clean Dishes, Clear Profits

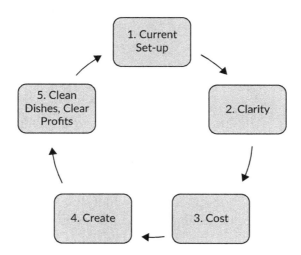

When the preceding four steps are followed, this next step becomes even more important. This step encompasses the snagging, ownership, training and maintenance of your new dishwash system. It covers the points that really make a difference and allows you to produce the results on the plates and onto the bottom line of your business.

Like anything new, there is a learning curve involved with your new dishwasher. Someone must be responsible for taking care of it and monitoring it to make sure that it is being used properly and to its fullest advantage.

Snagging

When you move into a brand-new house you typically have a full two years to report any defects or substandard workmanship. With a new commercial dishwasher system, the timescales will not be anywhere near as long, but you should be allowed at least a few weeks for the staff to get used to working with it and to report anything that doesn't seem right. This will be over and above the manufacturer's twelve months parts and labour warranty and should ideally have been addressed with your supplier in step two. This can be hard to implement in practical terms if you have bought a machine online with no real backup plan, but let's presume that you've bought it from the supplier that's looking after you throughout this process.

It is a general industry assumption that if something isn't quite right with the machine a few weeks after it has been installed correctly, then it must be down to user error and therefore chargeable. This can happen, but it isn't always the case. For example, the detergent might not be going in at the correct concentration for the new machine and the dishes are not being washed properly.

This is not the fault of the user, nor is it the fault of the installation engineer. Every restaurant is different in the food particles that need washed from the plates. During the commissioning of a machine, I tend to use the manufacturer default settings for the chemicals dosage as they are set at an industry standard, and when I know that they are being drawn in, I invite feedback from the customer after a week or two of use during full service. It can be a case by case basis as there are many chemical manufacturers on the market with different concentration levels.

I allow for this in our snagging so that we can revisit and fine tune the amount of fluid being fed into the machine to balance out chemical usage versus results. The concentration of good quality detergents and rinse aids normally need to be turned down.

There are instances when the user has made a mistake and caused the machine to develop a slight fault, ie not draining correctly. If there is anything causing a blockage, this would be a chargeable visit. However, with all new systems and machines that have involved changes of some sort, this brings along with it a learning curve.

In these instances, we allow for this and fix the problem. It involves some on-site retraining so that the staff understand what went wrong, how it went wrong, and what steps they must follow for it to not happen again. It's a metaphorical slap on the wrist not to do it again.

Our installation, commissioning, and testing of a new machine involves running through and completing a comprehensive checklist to cover as much snagging issues as possible. This includes tightening up hose clips, nuts, bolts and electrical connections that may have become loose in transit or making sure that the ribbon to control display panel is correctly in position and clipped tight.

That last example is a cracker because the machine appears to be totally dead and will not work, although the electricity is switched on. This is one that most people panic over because they think that they've just broken their brand-new dishwasher. It's easily rectified but I wouldn't recommend that you try this at home. Call your engineer back out.

Some of these machines have travelled thousands of miles from their respective factories and it's only natural to expect that there has been slight movement in machined parts. We try and cover as many bases as possible so that when your dishwasher is in active service and all pump motors have been vibrating away a few hundred thousand times (even in a matter of days), then this vibration does not cause anything else to come loose. Whatever the cause of the problem, and let's hope that it's only ever minor, remember to factor in some time for snagging.

Ownership

Your new dishwashing system is now in place. Awesome! Who is responsible for its daily, weekly, monthly and yearly upkeep to make sure that it lives up to its billing and performs to the max? Is it the owner, general manager, chef, or KP who is responsible for this task? I would say it's a bit of everyone, but mostly it's who has the time to properly look after it.

For example, on a daily and weekly basis, the KPs should be making sure that the machine is looked after and properly cleaned as it is operated. Make sure that at least on a weekly rota, someone is responsible for looking down the back and underneath the machine (depending on what type it is) and cleaning these areas. On a monthly basis there should be a deep clean that is signed off by the head KP, chef, or general manager.

Depending on the size of your place, most of these tasks may fall to one or two persons, and in small setups, the owner themselves may have to carry out this work. Regardless of who does it, it must be done and done correctly. Have this conversation with the installation engineer and whoever carries out the training for the machine.

Many chefs started their careers as a KP in the kitchen, taking on the responsibility of operating the dishwasher and making sure the dishes were clean. It's a great way to learn the ropes. Starting from the back and gradually working your way forward through the ranks towards becoming a head chef gives massive knowledge of what it takes to be involved in and run a busy kitchen. Being a KP, or 'the dishwasher' as many are known, is an honest and noble profession. It is hard work and rewarding. As part of a team, the KP is an important role and it must be viewed that way so that they are treated with the respect that every other team member is afforded.

When you have great KPs working with you, this is a step forward to 'sweating' your assets and getting the best out of your new dishwashing system. They are integral to its success. Formula 1 teams are filled with talented people who each know their role in the game at an intimate level. If the F1 management took little interest and didn't regularly train everyone involved, then metaphorically (and possibly literally), the wheels would soon fall off the car. Do not ignore the guys working in the background.

You will know more about this side than I will, however, when I see a successful team in action, it normally consists of a head KP, and a few other KPs that report to them. The head KP is the main person responsible for the upkeep of cleaning and operating correctly the dishwashing system.

Whether they do it themselves or delegate the cleaning out to someone, it needs to be scheduled so that it gets done on a consistent basis. This is the same when it comes to training the kitchen staff on how to keep the machine working properly and at its best. Regular training is key, and this is something that can be requested from the dishwasher manufacturer or supplier. Again, the head KP is the best person to monitor this and make sure that it is carried out, especially when new staff enter your workplace.

Training

All staff involved in the operation of the dishwasher should be fully trained in how to clean, operate, and get the best out of the machine and new system. Basic training should be given by the installation team when the new machine has been commissioned. This allows the staff to start using the dishwasher immediately. However, many customers will request that we return at a time that is convenient to carry out further training when all or most key staff can be present to learn how it should be used.

The best dishwasher manufacturers will allow for this and the local rep can be called in to help with training. These guys know their own machines very well and can provide nuggets of advice that can benefit the use and longevity that you will subsequently get from a new machine. Request extra training after six months to recap what the best practice with the machine is and to iron out any bad habits that have started to form.

Your staff should know the following basics:

- How to turn the water and electrical supply off
- Filling, operating (different cycles and why), wash, rinse, drain. Draining down, removing filters (only after draining down)
- Cleaning the machine, removing and cleaning the wash and rinse arms and jets, cleaning the filters, and then reassembling it all, ready for next service
- Understanding the dishwasher chemicals – which tube goes into which container, and how to safely change over from an old bottle to a new bottle

Back when I was a youngster, my dear old papa always lamented in how important your education was. 'Your education comes first!' was his mantra, and this has stuck in my mind and in the minds of my siblings and cousins throughout our lives. This was compounded by the fact that he was a school headmaster and that most of my aunties and uncles were teachers. So, the idea of lifelong learning was something that our family viewed with an open mind. It was in our DNA. If you don't already have it, I encourage you to adopt this mindset and let it permeate throughout your restaurant.

The more educated that your staff are on best practice for how to use your ware washers and how to keep them clean and look after them, the better that these machines will perform, and for much longer. Here are the main points that we cover when installing a new machine, or when speaking to staff about what they should and shouldn't be doing.

Empty out glasses and tumblers before placing upside down in the basket. Some people in a bar or a restaurant might think that they are doing you a favour by putting their used chewing gum in an empty glass, but if this gets inside your machine it becomes messy and difficult to clean. It catches on the filters and on the impellors of drain pumps and wash pumps. Hair and other particles builds up on these and they need to be cleaned out by an engineer as the pump can no longer rotate. Worst-case scenario is that the pump motor burns out and will mean a costly replacement.

If you have a sink next to your glasswasher, we recommend using this to empty out your glasses into. Place an old ice cream tub with small holes in it (to let liquid through) in the sink and your staff can empty glasses into that before placing them in the glasswasher basket. Some people even use a sieve suspended over a small sink. This collects all the debris, cocktail fruit slices, straws, etc, for disposal into your bin. This simple method protects your glasswasher and the sink plumbing from getting clogged up.

Another helpful thing for your staff to know when it comes to passthrough dishwashers is that some of them have a standby function at the hood. The hood can be lowered almost to close, but instead of closing it, it can rest a few inches open. It does not kick into a wash cycle and is great for retaining heat inside of the machine until it is ready to be used.

Regular training will help to ingrain these practices as habits. Keep in touch with your supplier or the manufacturer and train your staff well so that your machine will perform consistently better and you will get more years from it.

Maintenance

Regular Planned Preventative Maintenance programmes (PPMs) can minimise or even eliminate breakdowns. Ongoing checks by a reputable company, probably the one that you have used throughout this process, are a great idea to get the most from your machine throughout its life. When small problems are diagnosed and fixed before they become major faults, this takes massive stress away from the kitchen. The key here is prevention. Unfortunately, threaded throughout this book is the unpleasant theme that when your dishwasher or glasswasher breaks down during service, chaos normally ensues. You will know this first-hand and anything you can do in advance to reduce the chances of this happening should be carefully considered.

Most people have boiler and central heating cover at home because they understand how critical it becomes when their heating fails, or they run out of hot water. You may even have extended warranty on your television or washing machine. Hopefully you will have something similar in place to cover your dishwasher because you will want each service to run as smoothly as possible and your staff deserve to have that peace of mind. These plans will normally be a monthly retainer or payment that provides different levels of cover and are well worth looking into.

If you plan these service calls well, you can ensure that your staff can deep clean the area behind the dishwasher while the machine is out of position. Apart from some wear and tear repairs, when a decent dishwasher has been properly looked after by your staff and regularly maintained by professionals, it should perform the same after five years' service as it originally performed on day one of installation.

Now that you've read about the wash cycle steps and the theory behind what they do and how they work together, it's time to put them into action. When done correctly you will enhance and maintain the harmony between the kitchen, your staff, and your customers. There is a real positive knock-on effect that every business craves.

I get a real sense of achievement and feel great for our customers when they follow these steps and get positive results immediately. They are happy and their kitchen staff are delighted. It truly hammers the point home of how important this piece of machinery and its surrounding setup is to the guys on the front line that benefit from it. These guys are at their 'battle stations' for at least eight hours a shift so when they see it go from an underperforming bottleneck and frustration to become transformed into a sleek and finely tuned operation, their relief and joy is tangible. It's fantastic when we walk someone through this process and get to this point. It makes my work worthwhile.

CASE STUDY: STEPHEN SMART, HEAD CHEF AT THE MINT BAR AND RESTAURANT (NAVAN TAVERNS)

Stephen has over twenty-five years in commercial kitchens. He has been the head chef at The Mint for just over five years after starting off as a dishwasher and working his way through the ranks. He has a great knowledge of how the kitchen works from the bottom up.

There are many pieces of equipment and loads of elements that have to come together in a busy kitchen in order for the front end of your restaurant to work well.

In your experience, what role does the dishwasher play in all of it?

Stephen: *It's definitely one of the key elements and one of the most important because the bottom line is that if there are no clean plates then you can't serve your food. If* *we have no pots, pans and utensils then we can't cook the food. It helps to alleviate a great deal of pressure from our kitchen porters and chefs.*

Years ago, you were manual hand washing and the environmental health were on your back as you had to have a washing sink, a rinsing sink and a cool sink. It was a prolonged effort all day that increased your time and your labour in the kitchen.

The whole dishwasher system and that side of it is up there with your cookers, the fryers and the ovens. It's vital.

You have recently changed your dishwasher and tabling in your kitchen. What were your motivations for changing the dishwasher and setup?

Stephen: *Recently we have had a massive upturn in business following a refurb of the whole restaurant. This has increased our sales week on week, year on year.*

It was getting to the stage during service where waiting staff were having to place the dirty dishes next to the pass. There was a lack of space to set down the dirty dishes, so getting the gantry system with the new tabling has made such a difference. This alone means that we can get the food out a lot quicker and speed up our service.

We changed the machine itself due to the fact it had done its time and was at the end of its tether. We were getting to the stage that we were having to do two runs through the dishwasher to get one rack of plates through. It was constantly breaking down and costing us more every month to keep it going.

There was also the upheaval in the kitchen when it had to be repaired during service. You're working around the machine repair while getting absolutely hammered at lunchtime as your staff are in two small sinks trying to wash a load of dishes. All the while you're crossing your fingers hoping it's not going to break down again and then you're panicking every weekend thinking 'please let us get through this weekend'.

What information did you gather and what research did you carry out before deciding on a particular manufacturer and model?

Stephen: *I spoke to various people including yourselves, and I looked at the different supplier and manufacturer websites. When I did my research on certain models, you were finding that very rarely did these have to be fixed within the first few years and even after that. So, we're looking at five years before we're expecting anything major to go wrong with it.*

We worked out that the money we were spending each month on repairing and keeping the old machine going, means that we have a brand-new setup for the same amount of money, so it's paying for itself as well as taking some pressure off the payroll.

It is a large amount of money for a commercial dishwasher and tabling and you want to get it right at this stage. Were you aware of the different ways available for making payment?

Stephen: *To be honest the price did put us off at the start, but we did understand that we had to spend the money. We knew that if we went small, we would get small returns back. Could we have got away with a lesser machine, a cheaper option? Probably, but we would be two years down the line and fixing it a lot more.*

We had to go big, we had to go for a better dishwasher that was going to save us money in the long run and we knew we had to go for the best option.

I knew that there were different options. Especially when people are buying cars, and they're buying couches, sofas and so on, and you know there are different payment options there but whether or not its expensive APRs, buy now pay later, or it's interest free and I wasn't sure if they did that regarding catering equipment. We had to work out if the investment would cost us any more in the long run depending on how we paid for it.

Once a decision was made, what expectations did you have with regards to the removal of the old setup and installation of the new system?

Stephen: I was hoping that we were not going to find any problems as it was a bit of a weird setup we had in there before. I think the people that put it in were like John Wayne, a bunch of cowboys. I was panicking a bit hoping that we wouldn't find any problems and it turned out trouble free because the guys were very open to suggestions and they worked around us. The work was carried out the night before and then again at 7am the next morning and it meant that we didn't lose any service.

It was great from start to finish and such a relief not to encounter any major problems. It really helped us because we didn't have to close and we didn't have to turn anyone away as we rely on the footfall here.

Now that your new dishwashing system has been in a few weeks, what difference (if any) has it made?

Stephen: What a difference that it has made to the dishes! Before we were prespraying the dishes, putting them in the machine, then having to redo them to get most of the food off. We were having to change the dirty water in the machine on a busy Saturday around 6 or 7 times a day. We would have pots of boiling water on the stove to try and speed this up.

The new machine takes a bit longer to fill up because we don't use this method with it, but its quicker cycles and the dishes are clean, the baskets don't have to go through twice. We're also double stacking and putting through two baskets at the one time and they are coming out just as good, so it has saved us time. Again, we'll get a system in place and this might take us six months to a year before we're fully into our own way of working. We had eight or nine years working it the old way, and some people don't like change even if it is for the better.

What plans do you have going forward to get the very best out of your new system and sweat the asset?

Stephen: *Once we get Christmas out of the way, we'll get the manufacturer back out to go back over the machine again. The machine itself is quite self-explanatory although getting to grips with a new piece of equipment is tricky at first as staff a bit scared in case they break it! We realise that it takes a bit of time to get to know the machine and to get it working for you the best way that it can.*

Also, how organised we are in the kitchen is important. We could have the best dishwasher in the world but if we're not organised, it's not going to make much of a difference. Systems and processes are important. What I'll do is make up a setup plan with time ranges for morning and the rest of the day – what should be done by when.

We don't need to refill this new machine nearly as much so that's further time we've gained and the whole thing is night and day better.

In your experience where do your dishwashing system and your KPs fit into the grand plan of having satisfied customers in your restaurant?

Stephen: *Our industry is more about hygiene these days. When I look back it used to be 90% food based and 10% paperwork and hygiene. Now it's more 50-50 and more hygiene based because everyone can access your details online to check how good your rating is and how good your kitchen is.*

Your kitchen porters play a massive role and as I say it's the worst job in the world, one that I've done, and I'm still not scared to roll the sleeves up and get stuck in. I believe that we work well as a team and when someone is struggling we jump in and help them, but when you have that thankless job, that hard wearing job, you want to try and make it as easy for them as possible.

So when you've got a good dishwasher in place it can free up the KP to do other tasks. They don't have to keep checking for bits of food left on plates. They can get on with other things and it's boosted their morale because the job is easier for them now.

The plates are all coming out clean, going straight into the hot cupboard then ready to serve the food on and back out to service. There's nothing worse than having a nice plate of food served out to the customer and they feel under the plate and it has that gritty texture. That's what we had with the old machine. We don't have to worry about that anymore. The plates are coming out spotless, and the owner has commented about the difference in the plates and that's another thing we really wanted.

Stephen Smart, Head Chef at The Mint Bar & Restaurant (Navan Taverns), Coatbridge, North Lanarkshire

15
Follow The Steps

The flip side to all of this is when restaurants do it their own way and get it wrong. They do not give the process the proper attention it needs or cut too many corners and do it on the cheap. My methodology outlined above is by no means the only way to get this right, but it is the accumulation of years of experience in this specialist field that has led me to be able to spell it out in these five steps. Follow these steps and you will get it right. If you don't, then you might not get it right. Here's a look at a few things to consider that I come across when customers try and wing it and end up getting it wrong.

Excuses

Don't leave the dishwasher or glasswasher system as an afterthought or you will regret it. Unless you have done exceptionally well and pulled it out of the bag, you will be reminded every day by the way that the machine constantly underperforms and creates a bottleneck in your system. As well as that, your staff will probably be on your case every day with their (well justified) moaning. Don't wait until your last good members of staff are threatening to quit before you get it sorted. Act quickly. If you can't afford to buy a new dishwasher, then speak to your accountant and find out how you can obtain one. It is a sound investment and will make your life easier.

A cheap and cheerful dishwasher is rarely cheerful

Buying machinery purely on price can be a bad move when it comes to a dishwasher for your business. If you are remotely busy, remember that this machine will be the backbone of your food service. As I've mentioned, the dishwasher can be switched on in the morning and work solid with little respite all day until late evening. Your kitchen staff may change over after a shift, but your machine will be asked to keep hammering away. It is an industrial environment and you must spend the money that affords you to have a machine that is fit for purpose. If you buy cheap, you'll buy twice.

I deal with different types of venues and when it comes to this piece of advice, it means the exact same thing across the whole of the catering and hospitality industry. Let me tell you about how a golf club committee got this one drastically wrong. They had an old undercounter dishwasher that was on its last legs and was starting to let them down. It was a decent model that they had bought ten years earlier and they knew that it was time to buy a new one. They had already bought their glasswasher from us and it was a good little workhorse, so they asked us to quote them for a new dishwasher. We duly carried out the necessary work around this and worked out a price and buying options for a suitable model that we knew would fit their needs. However, they decided to buy the cheapest machine that they could find online. I present options so that they have a choice, and they have the choice to choose something else. That is absolutely their prerogative and I never begrudge anyone the right to make up their own mind. One of the members of the golf club installed the machine and that was that.

However, around four months later, we got a call from them to ask us to have a look at their new machine because it would not work. We obliged and discovered that the wash pump had burned out. There was nothing stuck in it, it had simply had enough and packed in. We relayed the problem and they telephoned the machine supplier while we were on-site. They were advised to send the faulty wash pump at their own expense to the UK address of the supplier so that they could assess it for a warranty claim. After a week of downtime, the golf club called up to find out what the state of play was. They were told that they shouldn't have sent the pump to them but instead they should have sent it back to Italy where the machine was manufactured.

At this point I would like to say that there are good Italian dishwasher manufacturers out there, some I have worked with for almost two decades. This, however, was not one of them. The golf club asked us to get involved again on their behalf and it was not an easy situation. This was a supplier that we hadn't used before. To cut a long story short, we ordered up a new pump at a cost of around £400 + VAT with a three-week lead time. We fitted the new wash pump and this cost included the initial call out, plus the labour. The money spent on the repair was only a small part of the overall cost, and the overall cost is something that people rarely see.

Golf in Scotland is a major pastime, regardless of the weather. You'll hear locals saying that in Scotland, there are only two types of weather: Cold rain and warm rain. That pretty much sums it up, although you must visit if you have never been – it's gorgeous. The folly of this golf club's decision unfolded in the middle of what was to be one of the hottest summers ever recorded when the fairways and greens were full, and the clubhouse was packed to the rafters every day. Any extra income generated on food sales was depleted on extra staff that had to stand and hand wash hundreds of dishes all day long throughout peak season. Also, because of the backlog in dishes, the food was not getting to the customers on time, which then created a drag in the service and took its toll on both the staff and the hungry customers. Several staff quit during this time.

The point I'm trying to make is, if it's a manufacturer that you've never heard of, then buyer beware. If you think that buying a good, reputable machine is expensive, then just wait until you buy a cheap one. You have been warned.

My dad will install it

So, you have bought a decent dishwasher from your supplier, but you don't want to pay the installation charge. You'll fit it yourself or get your dad or a friend to install it to save yourself some money. Before you say anything – no! It is not the same as installing a domestic dishwasher. Sure, it's water in, water out, and electricity. Should be simple enough. Again, no. This is a time-consuming and specialist job. It is rarely straightforward even for the expert and there is a great deal involved. This can end up being a false economy as you may have to call out a specialist service engineer to correct an install that has not been done properly.

If you buy online and things go wrong after a botched install, then it will cost more and there won't be any level of snagging involved with the purchase. A simple thing like making sure that the machine is properly levelled when in position will ensure that the door or hood opens correctly and does not run out of alignment. If this is incorrect it can break, thereby chopping years off a good machine.

You also run the risk of the staff not knowing how to properly operate and clean the machine. These points are covered when a professional installation is carried out. We've already discussed how important proper training is to get the best from your staff and their dishwasher.

Using an inexperienced company

I'm putting my own neck on the line here, but we've all got to start somewhere. Early on in my dishwashing career I sold a frontloading machine to a local church. It was a machine that didn't have the detergent pump fitted as standard, and this was an expensive option back then that they had decided to forgo.

Once I'd installed, tested, and commissioned the machine, I asked the church's women's committee to take a seat so that I could show them how to work and clean it. I was a bit wet behind the ears and before I started performing the demo, I used a pelican pump that I found under the sink, screwed it onto the top of a 5 litre of dishwasher detergent and pumped a few scoots into the darkened wash tank of the machine. This was already a naïve move on my part as I ran the risk of being splashed by the detergent.

As I conducted the demonstration, I had eight pairs of eyes staring at me and the pressure was on. They were all elderly women and they sat in a neat row facing me and each of them was excited at the prospect of getting to work this new shiny machine, but this was also mixed with a fair amount of scepticism as they couldn't see how this new-fangled piece of machinery could be as good as a pair of marigolds and hands in the sink method, that they had been doing all of their lives.

I started off by showing them how to turn the machine on and how it would fill up. As it took its time to heat up, we blethered about how things were moving on in the world and there were a few incredulous gasps as I told them the difference between a domestic dishwasher and this new commercial model. The fact that it could wash and dry the dishes in around three minutes left more than a few heads shaking in disbelief. It was time to put the machine into a cycle and we loaded up a basket and I had one of my lovely volunteers press the cycle switch for the first time since testing.

'Oh, listen to how powerful it is!'

'Wow, I'd love one of those in the house'.

'That's a smashing machine, son!'

I stood slightly in front and to the side of the machine with a smug look on my face. This was all good, I was loving the praise.

Then, I'll never forget how their expressions started to change and worried frowns appeared on each wrinkled face.

'Is it supposed to be doing that?'

I looked back at the machine.

'Aargh!'

There was white foam pouring out from under the door of the machine and down onto the floor. It started heading for the women who by this time were on their feet and making a retreat behind their seats with their arms flailing around.

I quickly switched the machine off and opened its door. Inside the cabinet was full of foam.

'Don't panic!' I shouted as I panicked. I just couldn't understand what had gone wrong. Then the penny dropped. I checked the pelican pump on the detergent bottle a little closer than before and could see small bits of green liquid on it this time round. Upon further investigation, I realised that the pelican pump really belonged to the 5-litre bottle of concentrated washing up liquid.

At least three lessons were learned that day:

1. Don't use an unidentified pelican pump from one chemical bottle on another bottle.

2. If you eat enough humble pie and say 'sorry' around 300 times, old people will forgive you, and might even see the funny side before you do.

3. Washing up liquid + commercial dishwasher = Foam Party!

Thankfully there was no damage done and although at the time I was inexperienced, I did have a good deal of product knowledge. You will be able to tell by yourself if a company is new to the market or someone is inexperienced, and it doesn't mean that they are bad at what they do. If they are honest and upfront with you and don't try to wing their way through the process, and if the package that they are offering is reasonable, then it might be worth giving them a go. Trust your gut on this one.

16
What You've Learned

I have taken you on a journey through your ware washing systems in your restaurant and I sincerely hope that you have found value in reading this book and that some of the real-life examples have struck a chord with you. Hopefully I have provided a few lightbulb and 'Aha!' moments along the way. If I have managed even once to make you think 'so that's why that keeps happening', and you are able to make a positive change as a result, then it has been a worthwhile exercise.

I urge you to share the knowledge within its pages with your staff, colleagues, and industry friends, so that they too can get the most out of their unassuming dishwashers. As a quick recap here are the Cs in my five-step wash cycle methodology again.

The five-step wash cycle methodology

1. Current Setup – examine in more detail what you have at present.

2. Clarity – around where your business is going, your dishwasher options and what else is available.

3. Cost – what budget have you allocated, and which finance options are out there?

4. Create – what to expect when a new system is chosen and is being installed.

5. Clean dishes, clear profits – the juicy bit. Training, maintenance, review, where it all comes together, and you can keep planning forward.

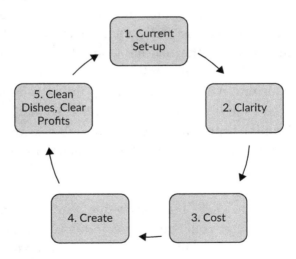

Having followed the five-step methodology, it leads you back to the beginning again. If you have done it right, it will mean that you shouldn't need to repeat this process for the same dishwash area for quite some time. Make sure that you review how your new 'current setup' performs, and regularly check that the process works to maximum efficiency. Look in on a regular basis and see how well it runs and have key members of your staff responsible for making sure that this happens, with accountability checks so that complacency does not start to creep in.

Concentrate on your dishwashing and glasswashing systems and it will pay dividends. With the help of your staff you can always refine and improve upon your systems and processes and continue to make marginal gains towards greater progress in your business.

I believe that your customers deserve clean dishes, and that you and the hard-working staff of your restaurant deserve clear profits. Good luck on your journey! If you would like to find out how your dish-washing systems perform now, and what impact they have on your restaurant, then take our scorecard at:

www.dishwashersandglasswashers.co.uk/scorecard

Afterword

The 6th 'C' – Contribution

If you think about it, you're in quite a privileged position. You may own your own restaurant or oversee one, and you are also educated to a high enough level to be able to read this book. However, not everyone or everything that we share our planet with are as fortunate as we are.

How often do you step back from the rat race and ask yourself what are you giving back as a business? Even if this is as simple as valuing your staff and letting them know that on a regular basis. But you can make a real impact on a much grander scale if you really put your mind to it. Profit does not just mean financial gain. There's more than one way to profit.

As a young child, whenever there was a wildlife programme on the television, my parents would call on me to join them and watch it as they knew that I loved animals, wildlife and anything to do with the natural world and our planet. It all fascinated me even although I was watching it in black and white. The soothing sound of the narrator transported me to wherever the camera was and throughout the years I recognised that this voice belonged to Sir David Attenborough. He is one of my heroes (the other being Billy Connolly), and I have grown up sharing his experiences and his wisdom on all things living, and I love his passion and attention to detail when describing his subjects.

It's no surprise then that more than thirty-five years later, I encourage my youngest son to watch wildlife programmes, documentaries, and videos that capture his imagination. I want him to live in a world that we can share with our fellow creatures, one where we all have an equal chance at survival over the next millennia. So, what can we do about it? We can make a start by consuming less of the available resources and contributing more back to help our planet thrive.

Energy, chemical, and water use are all on high consumption in a commercial kitchen. These can always be managed better and together we must take responsibility and consider the wider impact that using these resources has on our planet. Best practice moving forward is to have some sort of 'dishwash area management' in place. This should cover the machine, staff education and great habits, chemicals, waste segregation, and water reduction techniques.

As part of your regular review of your new dishwasher setup, keep an eye on how technology is evolving to help get us there. Tools such as blockchain, remote diagnostics, machine monitoring through connected technology and artificial intelligence are already making their way into our lives and into the kitchen and it won't be that long before it's all commonplace.

There is a global trend towards dishwashers becoming more conservative with their energy, chemical, and water usage and this is better for both your business and our environment. On September 25 2015, 193 world leaders committed to '17 Global Goals' to achieve three extraordinary things by the year 2030 (sustainabledevelopment.uk.org). The three aims are:

- End extreme poverty

- Fight inequality and injustice

- Fix climate change

The Global Goals for sustainable development can get these things done. In all countries. For all people.

As a responsible businessperson, I feel that it is our duty to get involved and to spread the word so that everyone can play their part. Because of the nature of my business, we have aligned ourselves with United Nations Global Goal Number 14 – 'Life Below Water', where we commit to conserve and sustainably use the oceans, seas, and marine resources for sustainable development.

We now create fantastic dishwashing systems for busy restaurants and kitchens that increase productivity, increase profits, and that are sustainable for our water ways, our oceans, and our world. Since getting involved, we have changed all of our dishwasher and glasswasher chemicals so that they are now more 'Machine, Water and World Friendly', in line with Global Goal 14.

And what does this mean exactly? It means that dishwasher components and internal parts should have a longer life as there are no acids in the rinse aids that attack plastics and no chlorine in the detergents to cause foaming, and further deterioration. Our rinse aids are also phosphate free which means that this will eliminate green algae growth in our waterways that build up and suffocate marine environments.

Our world is full of complex ecosystems that all rely on each other. When the oceans and water ways of the world thrive, it has a positive impact on land too. We want to get to the point where our chemicals and those used in every commercial kitchen are 100% environmentally friendly but do not compromise on the 1st class results that you guys need. Striking this delicate balance is not an easy task, although we will continue working with our suppliers to reach this point.

As part of your Environmental Policy, look them up and get involved. There are seventeen to choose from. It means that you and your staff can play your part in achieving the United Nations Global Goals for sustainable development of our planet: sustainabledevelopment.un.org

We aim to change our planet for the better, one commercial kitchen at a time, and we would love you to get involved and join us on our journey.

Make sure to connect with me.

Acknowledgements

Special thanks must go to:

My dad and Jane, and my mum. You always encouraged me to follow my dreams and to work hard for them. Mum, you know that flame will never go out.

My two sisters and brother, for always being there and putting up with my word count, and for millions of fantastic memories and laughs growing up (not there yet).

Cousins and close friends, for always providing laughs and a welcome escape; and for the rest of my family – we're a really close and fun bunch.

To the awesome customers that have helped to shape my character over the years. Learning at the coal face is the best possible way.

Thanks to Martin from Iceman Refrigeration – you kept me busy during the tough times at the start. To James, Tommy, Robert, Andy, and Simon – you guys were totally unselfish with your knowledge and saved my skin on multiple occasions.

I could never have discovered the content and concepts within this book if it wasn't for my fantastic work colleagues – Scott, Lindsey, and Gonçalo. The four of us must have lunch together some day.

My amazing and challenging children that help keep me focused on why I'm doing this. Amy and Jack for one reason, and Hannah and Lewis for a same but different reason. I finally did it, Pup.

And to my gorgeous wife, Gayle, the strongest and kindest person I know. Thanks for believing in me and putting up with my wild ideas. We'll get there.

The Author

Richard Hose is the Managing Director of Intellico Dishwashers & Glasswashers and works extensively within the catering industry, supplying commercial dishwashers to restaurants, cafés, the public sector, and other food and beverage establishments.

He gained a Bachelor of Arts Honours Degree in International Marketing with French after completing his degree year in France, having gone there with a very limited knowledge of the language. He also gained the equivalent French Diploma.

From a humble kitchen porter during his student years, through an 18-year career selling and repairing commercial dishwashers, Richard started up his own business in 2010 during one of the worst recessions in modern history. He has grown this business with the help of a small yet highly skilled team, and they pride themselves in 'Making Life Easier' for restaurant owners, chefs, kitchen and bar staff. They provide commercial dishwashing solutions to the catering industry that are sustainable for our waterways, our oceans and our world.

Richard is passionate about providing remarkable and sustainable solutions for his customers and is aiming to change the world for the better, one commercial kitchen at a time.

Richard is also a devoted husband and father.

⊕ www.dishwashersandglasswashers.co.uk

🐦 @WhichDishwasher and @Richy_Hose

🔗 Linkedin.com/in/Richard-hose-03a09661

CPSIA information can be obtained
at www.ICGtesting.com
Printed in the USA
LVHW081103230223
740234LV00021B/943